THE MOON FIX

THE
MOON
FIX

Harness Lunar Power
for Healing and Happiness

THERESA CHEUNG

Illustrations by INDIGO

WHITE LION
PUBLISHING

CONTENTS

Introduction
Talking to the Moon

Throughout time, humankind has gazed in awe at the heavens above, wondering about the eternal pageant of the stars and the meandering paths of the planets. But none of the celestial bodies, not even the sun, has inspired more myth and mystery than the moon.

Talking to the moon and listening to whatever she wishes to tell me has been my passion for as long as I can remember. From a very young age, it became a nightly ritual for me to sit on my bedroom windowsill and gaze at the moon before it was time to go to bed. On nights, when I couldn't see her shining clearly, I always felt a little lonely. During those nightly window-sill vigils, I would tell the moon everything I was thinking and feeling. I'd ask her to protect me and those I loved. Sometimes I would make a wish. I felt like she was listening to me. She felt alive. The moon lights and inspires every area of my life and helps me find a sense of direction and inner peace. She guides, protects and reconnects us with ourselves and our surroundings.

The moon fix recommendations in this book blend ancient and modern moon lore. They aim to help you immediately start harnessing or drawing down the power of the moon to give you the inner strength to change your life for the better. Every moon fix, whether it is a ritual, spell, meditation or practical advice, is simple and easy to do. Performing your moon fixes will help you to tap into the moon's energy at the optimum time of the lunar cycle to maximize your chances of success and happiness in every area of your life, every day of your life. *The Moon Fix* does not depend on astrology and New Age jargon, nor does it require any experience with magic, paganism or Wicca. You don't need to be religious or to have any belief system. All you need is an open heart and mind and a desire to tune into a higher power – the wisdom of the moon.

You'll find moon fixes here to improve your mood, heighten your creativity and improve your powers of concentration, as well as lunar recommendations to attract success, boost your energy levels and help attract love into your life or rekindle passion in a current relationship. There are also fixes designed to enhance your productivity as well as enchantments to ignite your intuitive powers and help you find your reflective and calm centre. If you want to live a limitless life and discover infinite possibilities within you, this book offers uncomplicated, practical ways for you to bring the transformative magic of lunar power into your everyday.

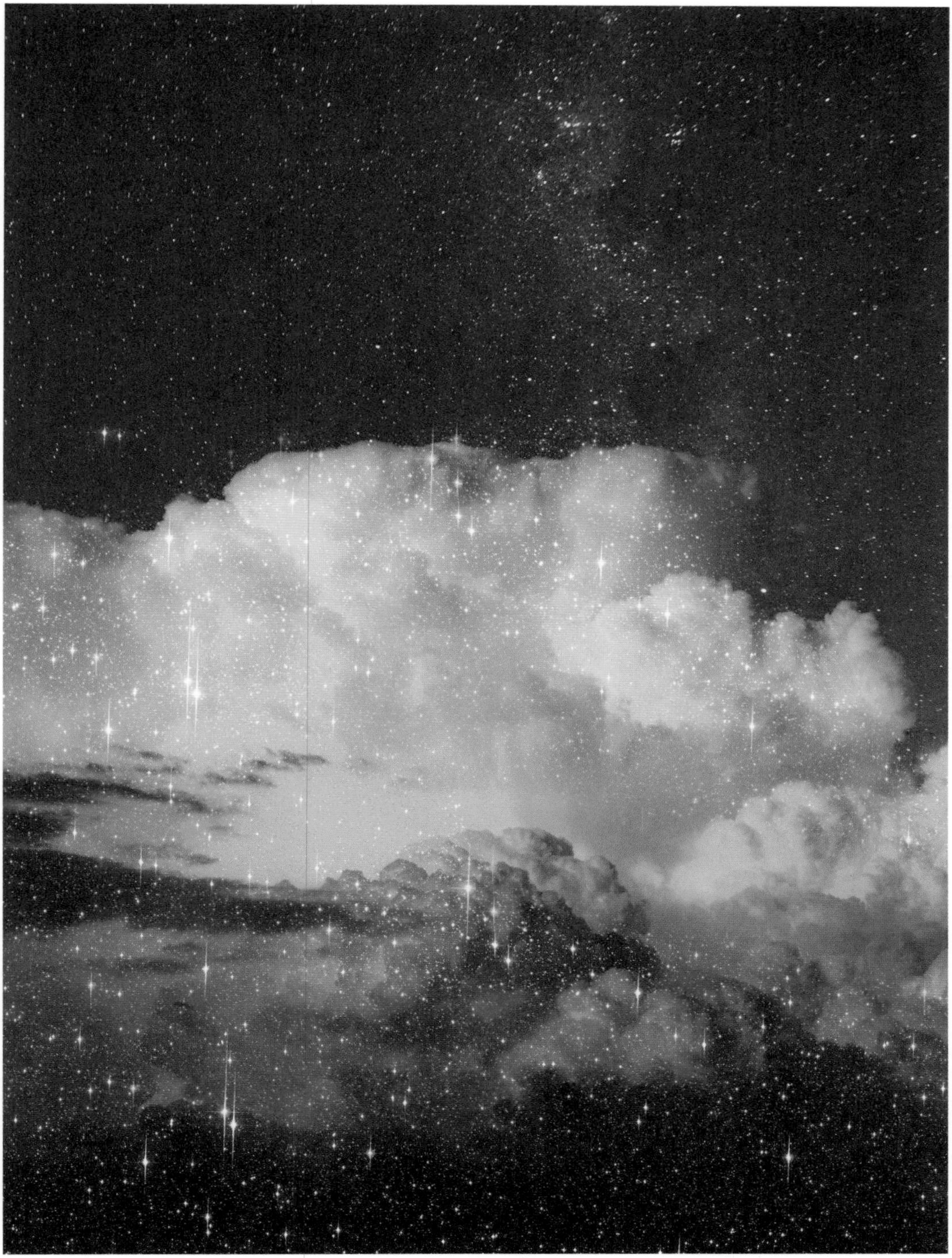

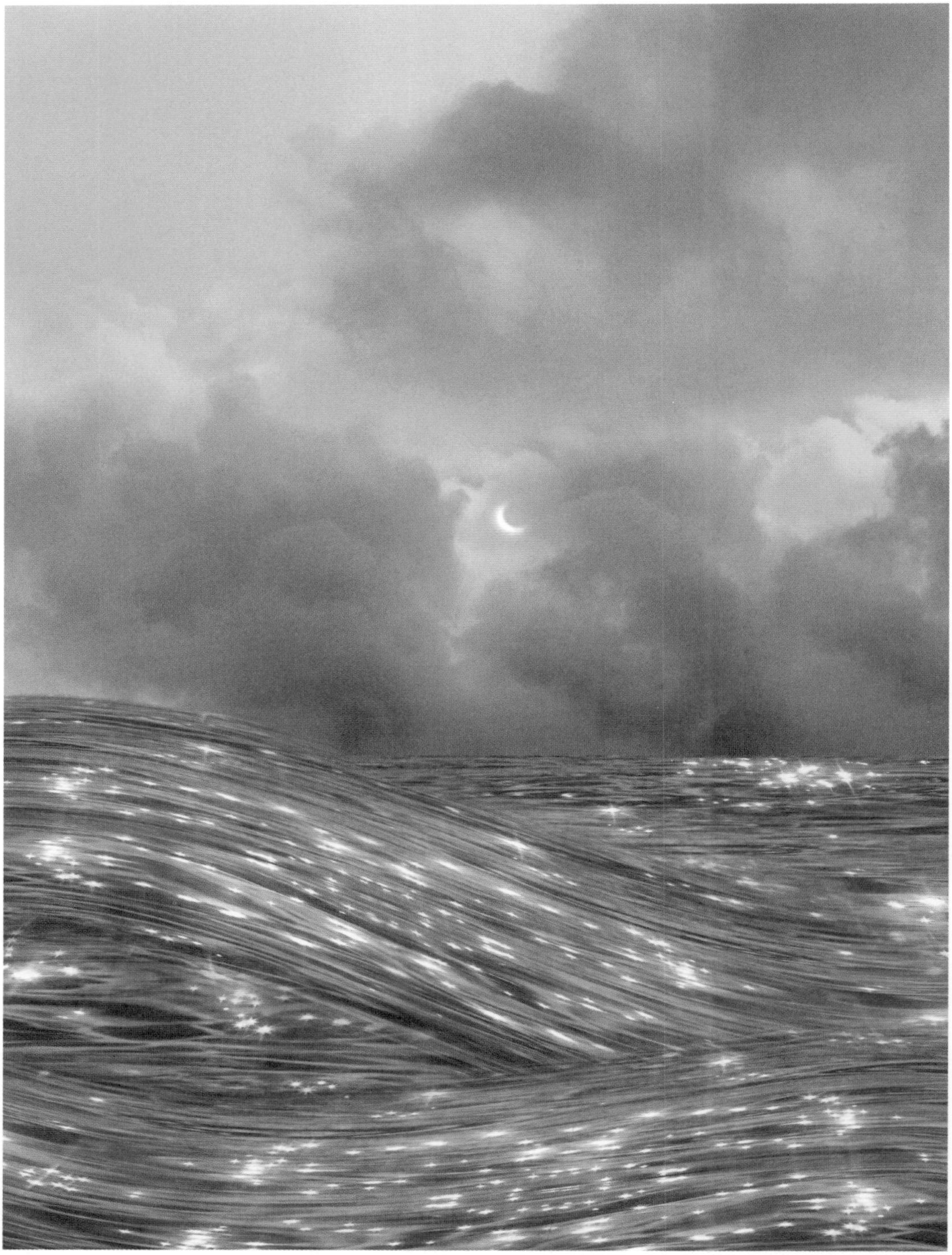

The Healing Power of the Moon

The healing power of the moon is a part of the mythology of ancient cultures and civilizations from all over the world, from the Greeks, Romans, Egyptians, Sumerians and Chinese to the Norse, Celts and Native Americans, to name but a few. Each culture has different moon lore, and names and ways to describe the moon and her many phases. More often than not the names given to the moon during her different phases recorded the flow of time, but sometimes they reflected the wild, magical legends and lore about the creation of the moon. Most cultures believed the moon to be a feminine energy, and this book will use the feminine to reference her, yet according to Norse mythology, the moon's energy was masculine.

Even when they appeared to hold fundamentally different beliefs about the moon, many ancient cultures were united by the firm conviction that the moon had significant power, both in the night sky and over our daily lives. Scientists and spiritual seekers today also recognize this.

So why and how does the moon influence our lives? The answer lies in the close and intertwined relationship that the moon has with the Earth in space. Most of us know that the moon's lunar phases somehow impact the tides, and science has shown that the gravitational pull of the moon on the Earth impacts not just the oceans but the climate, the temperature, the seasons and the weather too. In addition, without the moon's stabilizing influence the Earth would be spinning way too fast for us to survive. In short, we need the moon up there in the sky looking down on us day and night to keep us balanced and, it seems, alive.

Everything in the universe is energy and that includes you, me and the moon. I believe that tuning your personal energy in to lunar energy by becoming aware of the moon's many faces and phases can have a healing and balancing impact on all areas of your life. From starting new projects when the moon is full, to attracting love and success when the moon is waxing, or getting fit and losing weight when the moon is waning, working with the healing power of the moon is a powerful way to create positive shifts in all areas of your life.

Divine Principle

There are moon deities in every culture and they are typically linked to enchantment and magic. In the great majority of cases moon deities are feminine entities, queens of the night; however, the moon has been worshipped both as a heaven man and a heaven woman, and there are certain energies associated with it which are typically regarded as either feminine or masculine. These qualities do not apply exclusively to any particular gender. Harnessing lunar power is for everyone – it speaks to the hidden, mysterious and intuitive parts of a person.

TRY THIS For goddess meditations to awaken three different aspects of the sacred feminine, see Invite Courage from the Maiden Goddess, page 143; Find Nurture from the Mother Goddess, page 144; Seek Reflection from the Wise Woman, page 147.

Feminine and Masculine Principles

The moon is most commonly given feminine attributes, often referred to as 'she'. With the lunar phases typically lasting around 29 days, perhaps not surprisingly women have always had a unique connection to this powerful part of our night sky. Women's menstrual cycles are believed to follow the rhythm of the moon. The very words 'month' and 'menses' are ultimately from the same root as 'moon', and the waxing, full and waning phases correlate to the three phases of the menstrual cycle, with the full moon associated with ovulation and the waning with bleeding. However, feminine qualities are not exclusive to women and can apply to everyone. Such qualities typically associated with the moon include: reflection, presence, intuition and mystery.

As mentioned previously, in some ancient belief systems the moon was not considered a feminine but a strong masculine force. In Norse mythology, for instance, the moon is masculine and called Mani. Action, drive and momentum are typically regarded as key masculine principles of the moon, but again they can be gender non-specific.

Triple Goddess

An aspect occurring over and again in mythology was the notion of divine triads: three linked gods or one god with three distinct aspects. Perhaps this strange convention was a reference to the major phases of the moon – new and waxing; full; and waning. It may also be connected to the notion of the three stages of woman. The new and waxing moon typically symbolizes the divine feminine archetype of the maiden, the full moon is usually associated with that of the mother and the waning moon with the wise woman or crone. A modern mythic take might add a fourth stage of womanhood – the enchantress. This is the fully sexual woman who is independent from the mother. It is her power that is unleashed by the ripe full moon.

An example of this can be seen in Greek mythology in which three goddesses associated with the moon – Artemis, Selene, Hecate – could each be seen as representing these three distinct aspects of the sacred feminine (maiden; mother; crone).

How to Use This Book

The Moon Fix is a modern guide to working with the moon, offering a unique insight into how to align yourself with the phases of the moon and harness the energy of those phases. You should use this book as your holistic guide to discovering the physical, emotional, mental and spiritual benefits of incorporating an awareness of the moon into your daily life.

Living with the Moon

The first chapter provides an introduction to the phases of the moon and how these phases can govern your emotions and innermost motives. Although this book does not depend on astrology, you will find out about the significance of the moon travelling through different zodiac signs and the impact of other lunar effects on your daily life.

Working with the Moon

The second chapter will show you how you can harness lunar power to manifest and celebrate your deepest desires. You will be encouraged to follow the moon every day, so you know when it is optimum for you to work with her. You will also learn how to keep a daily moon journal, create your own moon altar and discover which crystals, incense, herbs and oils are best for your moon work. And if you have ever fancied a spot of full-blown moon bathing, there's advice about the illuminating and healing benefits of that here, too.

Getting Your Moon Fix

The heart of the book is Chapter 3: Your Moon Fix. Presenting 48 unique moon exercises and rituals, they are organized into subsections, arranged according to key life areas, such as love and relationships or health and wellness, to help you create a holistic lunar life plan. You can also turn to the Index of Fixes by Need at the back of the book, which identifies common emotional needs or life situations for which you can draw down the healing power of the moon (for example, if you have a broken heart or have an upcoming interview), and directs you to the most appropriate moon fixes for that specific need.

Throughout the Book

You'll find recommendations to perform a moon fix during a particular phase of the moon or when it is passing through certain zodiac signs – to help you synchronize with their specific energies. The following websites have options to choose which country you are in, and will help you check where the moon is in relation to you:

Moon phase: www.timeanddate.com/moon/phases
Moon sign: www.mooncalendar.astro-seek.com

CHAPTER 1

LIVING WITH THE MOON

The notion that the rhythms of the moon can govern your emotions and motivations is an age-old belief. In this chapter, we explore the main phases of the moon and just what impact they have on our daily lives.

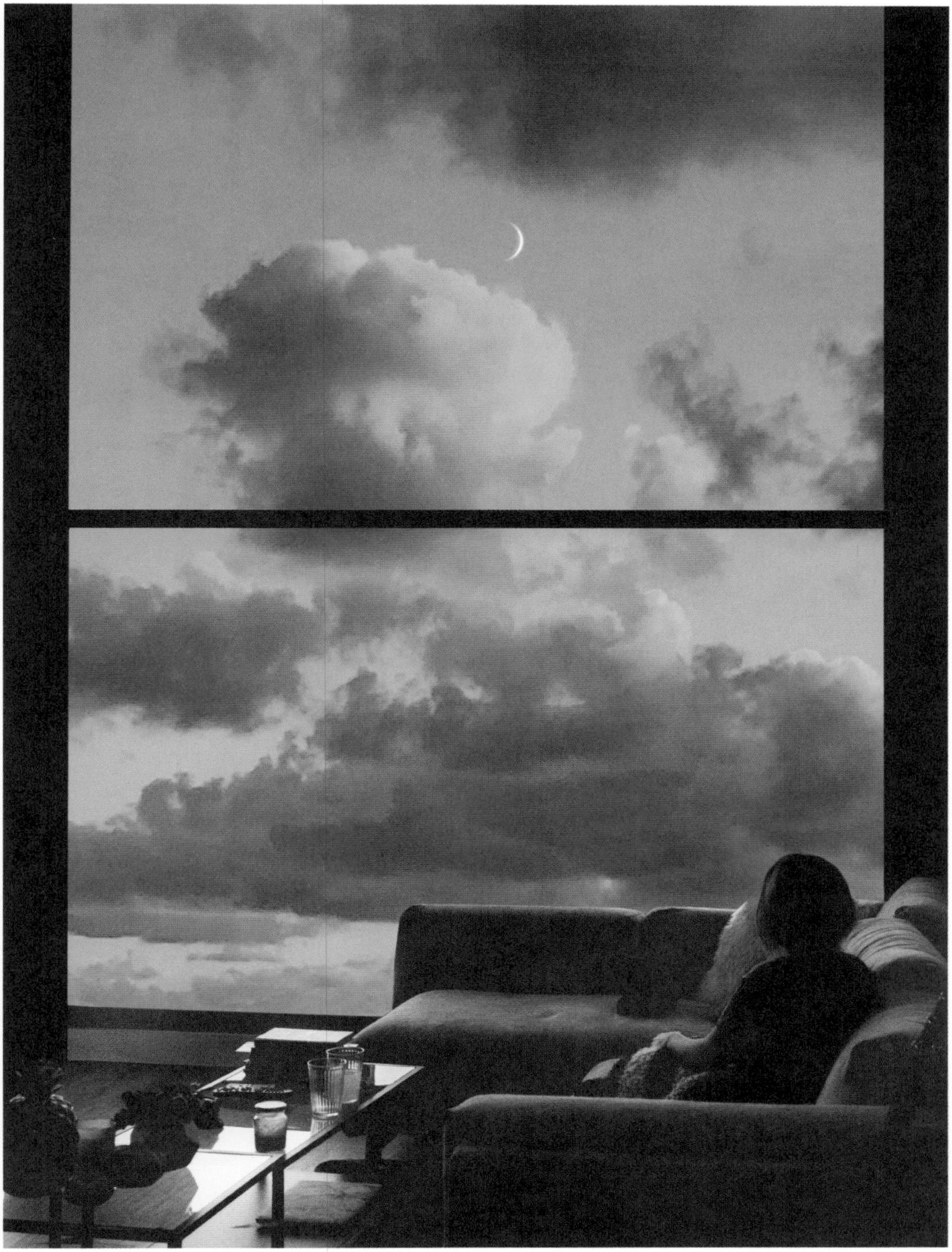

Phases of the Moon

This book will focus on the four major phases of the moon and show you simple, natural ways to tune in to and honour those phases. Every month, or approximately every 28 to 29 days, the moon will move from new to waxing to full to waning without fail, and each of these phases has its own particular magic. Every phase of the moon really can impact your mood, body and life.

There are also other intermediate and lesser-known phases of the moon, which each have their own energy. However, awareness of the four main phases outlined above is all you really need to strengthen your magical connection to the moon.

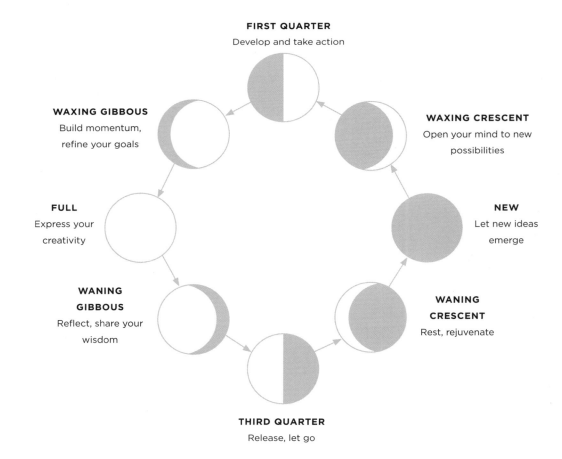

FIRST QUARTER
Develop and take action

WAXING CRESCENT
Open your mind to new possibilities

NEW
Let new ideas emerge

WANING CRESCENT
Rest, rejuvenate

THIRD QUARTER
Release, let go

WANING GIBBOUS
Reflect, share your wisdom

FULL
Express your creativity

WAXING GIBBOUS
Build momentum, refine your goals

New Moon

NEW BEGINNINGS

The new moon is sometimes called the crescent moon. It's when you can only see a glint of her illumination in the sky, if you can see her at all. During this phase, the moon sits directly in-between the sun and the earth, and the earthward-facing side of the moon is entirely unilluminated (the dark moon) or only partially illuminated so we cannot see her clearly. The absence of light during this phase can feel unsettling but, if you embrace the darkness, you can understand that it can be a doorway to possibility – the energy contained in intentions which is about to manifest.

NEW MOON ENERGY

The new moon is a time of darkness and pause. It embodies the essence of beginnings, the research, pause, preparation and planning that sets everything in motion. The new moon phase can also be seen as a time for the beautiful feminine qualities of reflection and presence to come to the fore, rather than the masculine principles of action and drive.

NEW MOON WORK

Use this phase for goal setting and making positive changes that can be developed later. Whatever is left undone or has gone awry during the previous lunar cycle, you now have the opportunity to accept – this is your chance to learn from your mistakes, begin again and start anew.

- **REST** Treat this as a time for rest; put your energy into self-care.
- **PAUSE** Refrain from making big decisions or purchases.
- **DETOX** Take a cleansing bath by candlelight. Add sea salt or Epsom salt to your water for their detoxifying effects.
- **CLEANSE** Use aromatic herbs and aromatherapy oils, such as sage and lavender, to clear the atmosphere of your home.
- **CONNECT** Sit or walk outdoors at night to open yourself up to new ideas promoted by moon energy. Make sure you are in a safe, well-lit area.
- **UNWIND** Keep lights low in the evening and try to avoid screens.
- **PROTECT** Wear or meditate on dark, protective crystals, such as smoky quartz or lapis lazuli.
- **MEDITATE** Spend time in quiet inward-looking activities: meditation, deep breath work, journalling, and on rituals. Treat yourself to a massage.
- **REFLECT** Pay special attention to your dreams, which may have a message from your deepest self. Write them down as soon as you awaken.

Waxing Moon

TAKING ACTION

The waxing moon is the phase when the angle between the moon and the sun increases. The moon begins her movement from being virtually unseen at new moon to being completely visible at full moon. Each night, she reveals more of her beauty and magic. It can feel reassuring to see the moon grow in visibility and to witness her strength and power returning. After the darkness, new light dawns again and this new hope inspires us to move our intentions from the unseen world of possibility to the visible world of positive action.

WAXING MOON ENERGY

The waxing moon period is a time for determination. It encourages you to make decisions and commit to putting your best-laid plans into action in the direction of your goals. It is time to water the seeds that have been planted so they can grow. The waxing moon is a moment for the masculine principle of drive to balance the feminine principle of reflection.

WAXING MOON WORK

Aligning yourself with the increasing energies of the waxing moon, you can use this phase to focus on whatever it is that you want to attract more of into your life – be it love, money, relationships, healing or courage – and then take appropriate action.

- **ACT** Be proactive and productive; put your energy into self-discipline and persevering.
- **EMPOWER** Strengthen relationships and use this time to deal with business and financial matters.
- **FOCUS** Use aromatic herbs and aromatherapy oils to help you concentrate and focus better. Bergamot, wild orange, peppermint and basil can all rekindle your drive.
- **MOTIVATE** Connect to waxing moon energy by reading motivational quotes every day.
- **ENERGIZE** Wear or meditate on energy-boosting crystals, such as clear quartz, jasper or garnet.
- **REFLECT** Light an orange or a yellow candle (energy-giving colours) – and review your life goals by candlelight.
- **EXERCISE** Spend time being more physically active than usual.

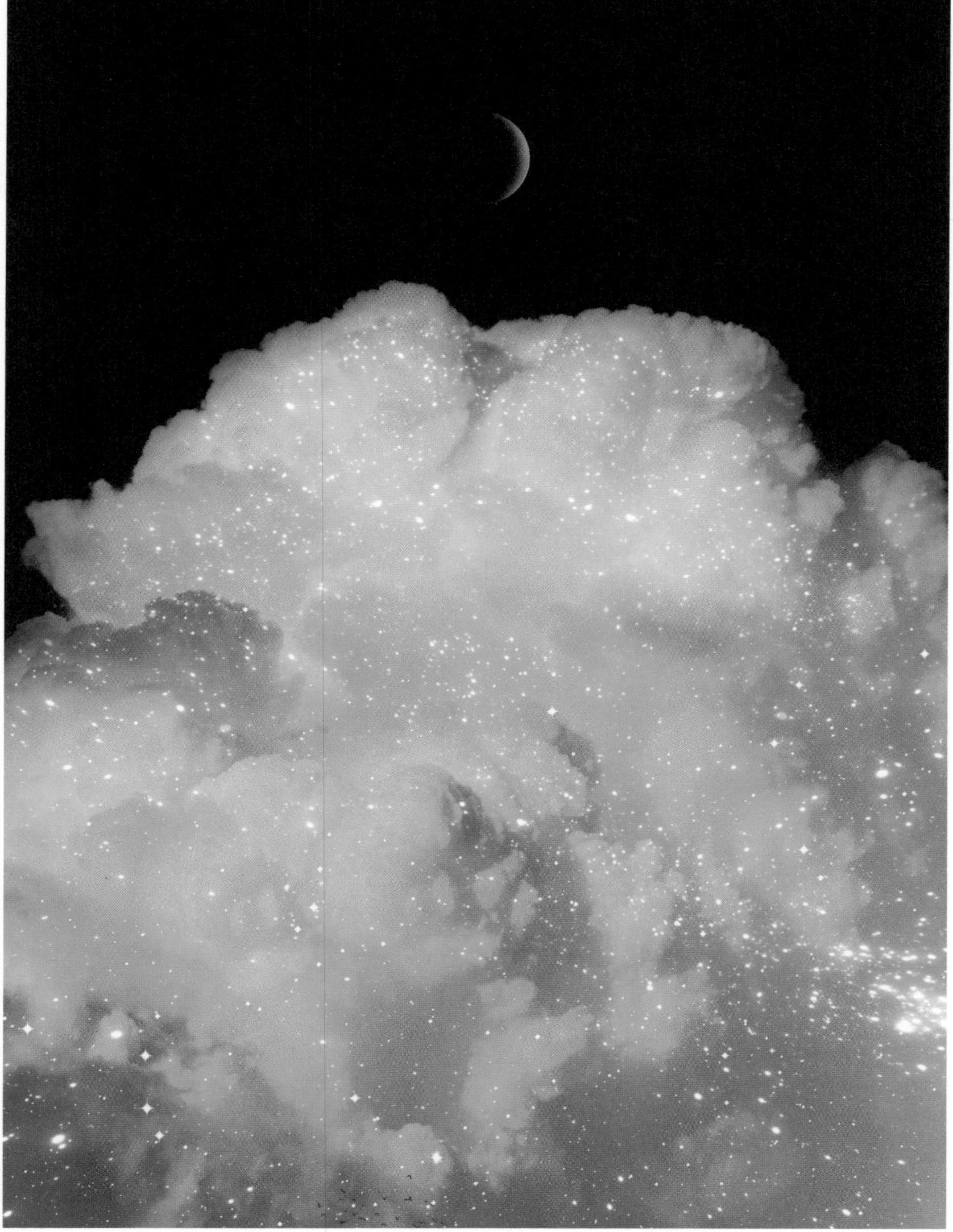

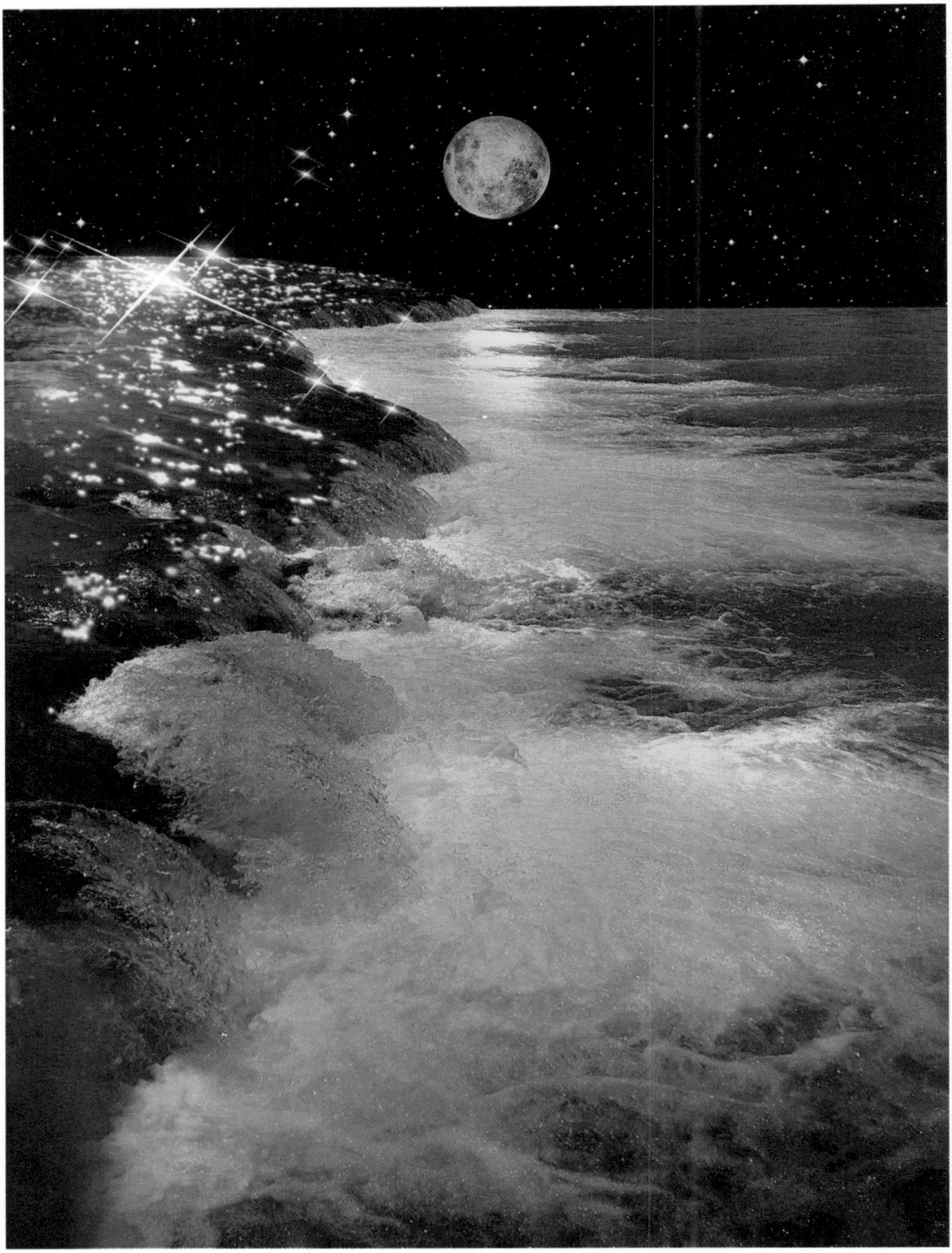

Full Moon

HEIGHTENED CREATIVITY

The full moon is the most powerful phase of the lunar cycle. It usually happens between 15 and 18 days after the new moon. During this phase we see the moon fully illuminated by the sun as a perfect circle in the sky with a beautiful glow radiating towards us. This is the culmination of the moon cycle, the point when lunar energy reaches its peak. We often feel its effects as increased sensitivity and charge – which is why the full moon has been associated with lunacy (from the word 'lunar').

FULL MOON ENERGY

Instinctively, we feel this is a time for dreams to come true and for there to be celebration and fulfilment. However, the full moon's intensity can sometimes bring an increased risk of anxiety and stress. Everything feels heightened during this phase and emotions come to the surface. When we recognize our feelings for what they are, we can channel this energy and use it to embrace what truly serves us and discard what does not.

FULL MOON WORK

The full moon reveals the full power and glory of the sacred feminine energy. With lunar energies at their most abundant and flowing, this is the perfect time to perform moon magic or rituals. It is the ideal time to celebrate your successes, let go of any bitterness and regrets, and fill yourself with gratitude.

- **REFLECT** Focus on positive feelings and what and who you have to be grateful for in your life.
- **RELEASE** Shine a bright light on what is blocking you; let go of what is holding you back; invite what is lacking into your life.
- **CELEBRATE** Plan a party or treat yourself to something.
- **FORGIVE** Let go of any anger or bitterness you have towards others.
- **UNWIND** Walk under the light of the moon. Let mother moon shower you with her love.
- **REVEL** Give your partner a massage or treat yourself to a candlelit bath.
- **DESIRE** Wear or meditate on passion-boosting crystals, such as opal and ruby.
- **CONNECT** Burn sage and tell the moon you are releasing all negativity. Connect with mother moon via a goddess meditation (see page 144).
- **EXPRESS** Pour out your feelings and your creativity in a journal.

Waning Moon

RELEASE AND RESOLVE

The waning moon is when the moon begins to decrease its angle from the sun and decreases from full to dark or new again. After the high point, with the full moon lighting up our energies, the waning moon can sometimes feel like an anti-climax, but it is perhaps the most significant of all the moon's phases. This is when the moonlight shines most brightly on the vital importance of completing tasks, as well as releasing what is unwanted. What we do during this phase of the moon will often determine the success of all the other phases.

WANING MOON ENERGY

The waning moon reveals the moon's natural instinct to always restore balance and harmony in our lives. Living life in the fast lane all the time will eventually lead to burnout and reckless behaviour. So, the decreasing moon is a signal for us to take the time to breathe, relax, accept ourselves for who we are, and to heal and dream.

WANING MOON WORK

The waning period is the time to reflect, learn and stay on track. It is also the perfect time to completely release from your life whatever or whoever is holding you back or no longer serves you. This could be relationships that have grown toxic or habits that are destroying your health.

- **PERSEVERE** Don't give up now. Keep going and complete projects.
- **REFLECT** Think about all that you have learned and share your wisdom with others.
- **CLEANSE** Tidy up your home and work space. Tidy up your lifestyle by quitting bad or unhealthy habits.
- **SUPPORT** Offer to help someone. Do some volunteer work. Be of service to others.
- **CONNECT** If you have a pet, spend more quality time with them than usual.
- **REFRESH** Spend some time in the outdoors to recharge.
- **HEAL** Wear or meditate on calming and healing crystals, such as amethyst or jade.
- **RENEW** Commit yourself to moving on and going forward with your life. Remember a new moon – and therefore a new beginning – is close by.

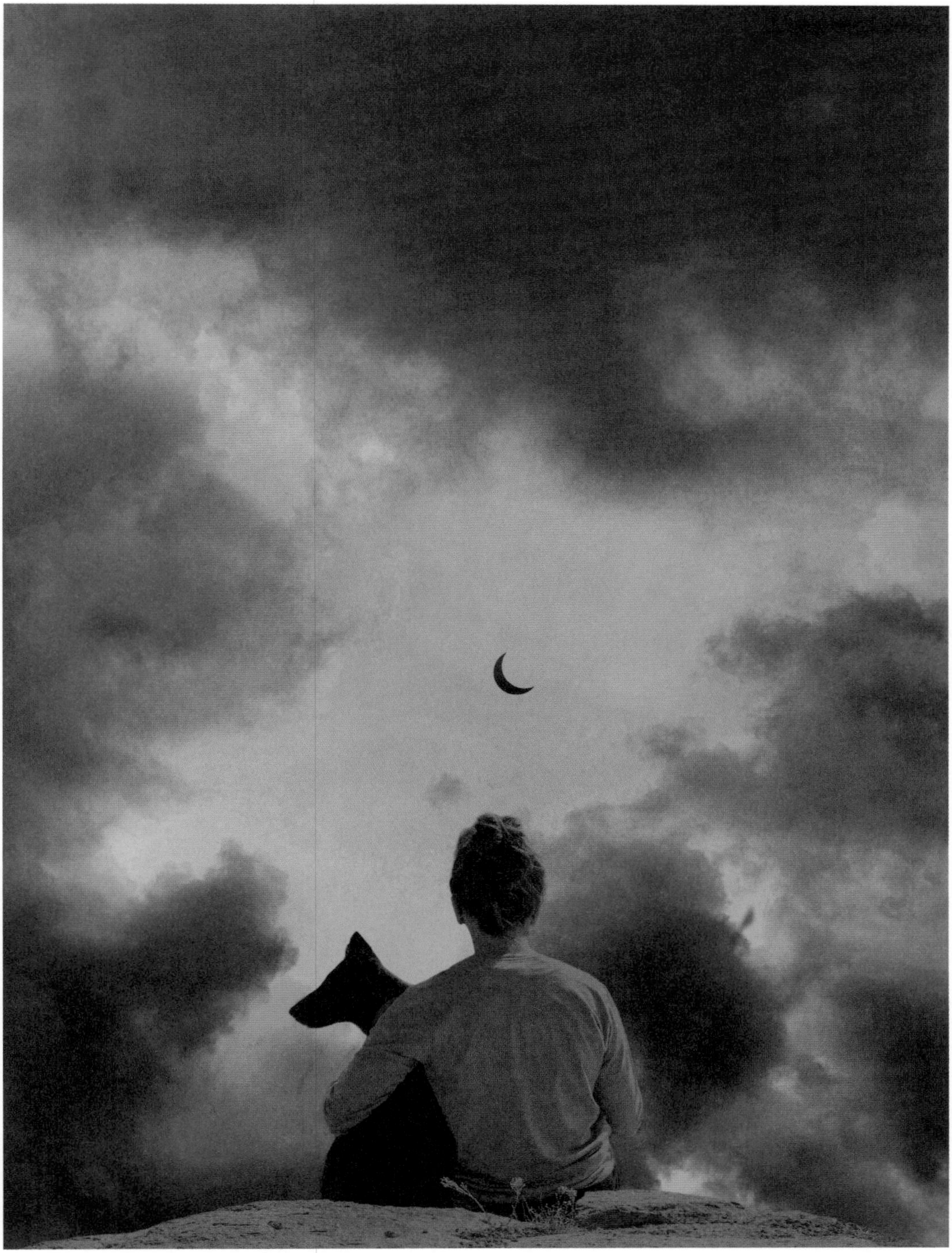

Moon Signs

According to astrologers, the sign the sun was positioned in when you were born reveals your character, and maybe even your fate or destiny. Even if you don't believe in astrology, you probably know what your sun sign (aka star sign) is and perhaps you have often marvelled at how accurately that sign describes you or aspects of you. Unless you are an expert astrologer you may not realize that astrologers also take into account the position of the moon and other planets at the time of birth to reveal deeper aspects of a person's character. Whereas your sun sign represents the outer you or the way you present yourself to others, your moon sign describes the inner or real you. If you are interested in researching further and discovering your moon sign, see the reccomended website on page 173.

No matter what your sun or moon sign is, it is important to point out that the moon travels through different astrological signs every few days. Every sign it travels through brings its own energies and influences that can work either for or against you, so knowing which sign the moon is currently in can further enhance the power of your moon work. Outlined on pages 26–29 is a brief guide to the influences each sign brings when the moon is travelling through it. As the moon enters each new sign, the characteristics often linked to that sign are more likely to manifest.

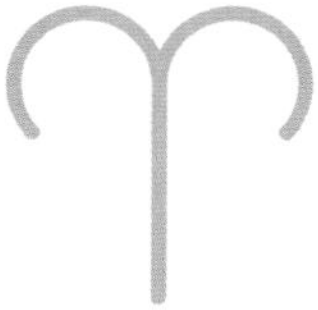

ARIES

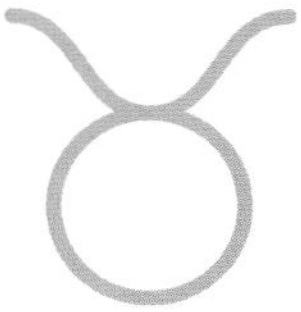

TAURUS

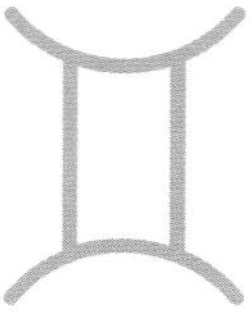

GEMINI

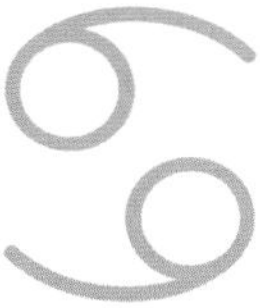

CANCER

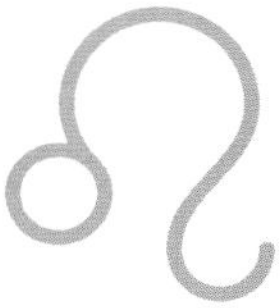

LEO

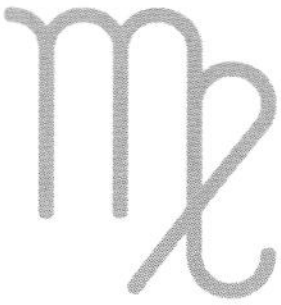

VIRGO

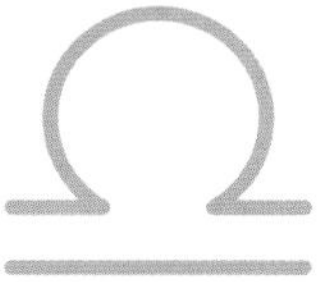

LIBRA

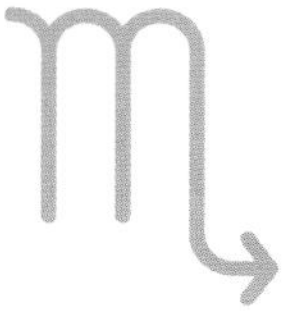

SCORPIO

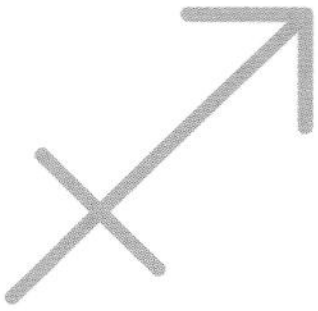

SAGITTARIUS

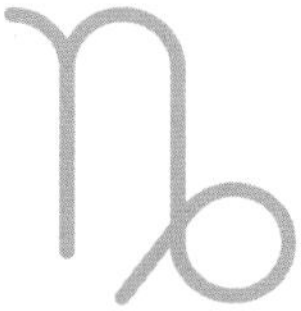

CAPRICORN

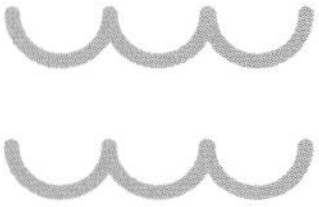

AQUARIUS

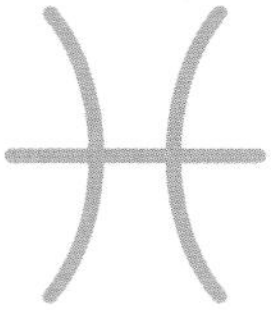

PISCES

Moon in Aries

New beginnings and taking action are centre stage when the moon is in Aries. Courage, initiative, leadership, originality, spontaneity and challenge are all key words. It's a time for you to have fun, take risks, enter competitions, apply for jobs, start a new hobby, hog the limelight and state your case. Travel, physical exercise and outdoor adventure are also favoured during this time. The focus is on short-term rather than long-term goals. Avoid becoming too self-centred during this fiery moon phase. It's also a time to keep your emotions in check and not let them control you. Learn to consider other people's feelings.

Moon in Taurus

Stability and inner calm are under the spotlight when the moon is in Taurus. Emotional security, charm, consideration, consistency and feeling grounded and relaxed are all key considerations. It's time for you to be reliable and responsible, to really think about what you want to achieve in life and to consider what matters most to you. This period highlights sensuality and artistic talents and time spent in nature, and it is also a good moment to invest, upgrade, redecorate, reorganize your finances and think about your retirement plans. The focus is on long-term stable relationships. Avoid becoming stubborn and indulgent and learn the importance of going with the flow and letting go of grudges.

Moon in Gemini

Communication is a firm focus when the moon is in Gemini. Intellectual stimulation, entertaining, flexibility and keeping an open-minded interest in the world around you are key influences. It's time for you talk to yourself and others with honesty. This is the time to concentrate on learning and study, writing speeches and starting new projects. New ideas and travel are favourable during this time and it is also a good time to make friends and meet new people. The energy of this moon phase lends itself well to upgrading everything in your life, from your phone to your self-care routine. Avoid superficiality at this time and if you suffer from a short attention span learn the importance of seeing things through to the end.

Moon in Cancer

Issues surrounding home and family come to the fore when the moon is in
Cancer. Emotional management, intuition and psychic development are all
strong influences. It's the ideal time to set your intentions and embark on
a personal development programme. Home improvements and long-term
romantic commitments are highlighted and it is also a good time to focus on
what your feelings are trying to tell you. Anything to do with home life and
domesticity lends itself well to this moon phase. Avoid being oversensitive to
criticism and overly protective to those you love. Learning to take yourself less
seriously and to enjoy life more will help you flourish.

Moon in Leo

Self-confidence and self-expression are in the spotlight during this phase.
Friendship, reinvention, generosity, creativity, charisma and celebration come
to the fore. It's time for you to lead and to enjoy rather than fear that feeling
of power. Love, laughter, indulgence and extravagance are key during this
time, so parties and any kind of social gathering are likely to be a hit. Holidays
and spoiling yourself are also recommended but avoid overindulgence;
boastfulness and arrogance are traits to hold in check. Learn to see through
the flattery of others and draw inner confidence from your sense of self-worth
rather than the praise or admiration of others.

Moon in Virgo

When the moon is in Virgo pay close attention to the details of your life.
Serving or helping others is another powerful influence that favours the moon
in Virgo. It's the perfect time to take stock of your life and to reorganize your
priorities. It's also a great period to focus on improving your health and to
take a close look at your diet and exercise routines, as well as making sure you
are getting enough sleep and have effective stress-management techniques
in place. Although getting yourself organized and tidying up are favourable
activities, you should also think about ways to help, teach, serve or inspire
other people. Avoid being overly fastidious and serious and watch your
tendency to worry about what other people think.

Moon in Libra

Beauty, the arts, harmony and companionship are centre stage right now. Partnership, negotiation, justice and cooperation are key influences. It's time for you to pay attention to partnerships of any kind and focus on ways you can be more diplomatic. If anything in your life seems unbalanced right now, see if you can find a way to rebalance the scales while the moon is in Libra. This particularly applies to relationships and making sure that one person isn't doing all the giving or all the taking. Surround yourself with peace, tranquillity and beauty during this time. Pamper yourself and avoid unpleasantness and indecision as much as possible.

Moon in Scorpio

Intensity, passion and focus are highlighted when the moon is in Scorpio. Everything will feel heightened emotionally and there will also be a focus on mystery and sexuality. It's the perfect time to focus all your attention on a project or a relationship and to make sure you are in control of what is happening in your life. It's also a good period in which to make decisions or big changes in your life and to avoid temptation, jealousy and irritability. Although this is an intense time, avoid taking yourself too seriously and try to let go of any grudges. Spend time working on those parts of yourself that you feel least comfortable with.

Moon in Sagittarius

The moonlight shines on freedom and optimism when it is in Sagittarius. Travel and holidays are favoured, as is study or taking up a new hobby or interest. It's also a time to reflect philosophically on what really matters to you in life and what you feel the true meaning of your life is. Laughter, risk-taking and approaching life in an adventurous open-minded way are key influences. This period is ideal for thinking about all you have to be grateful for in your life and, if you tend towards negative thinking, to counteract that with a more positive mindset. Avoid being irresponsible and tactless, and appearing superficial.

Moon in Capricorn

Responsibility, hard work and reserve are your defining characteristics when the moon enters Capricorn. Efficiency and ambition are other key influences. It's time to dream less and take a more down-to-earth and practical approach to life and to put in the hours needed to advance your dreams. If you work hard and remain determined, your chances of success in your career or work will improve. It is the perfect moment to showcase your personal self-discipline and willingness to go the extra mile. Avoid becoming overly cynical, controlling and rigid in your thinking. Nothing can hold you back but your own pessimism and lack of flexibility.

Moon in Aquarius

Originality and flair define the moments when the moon is in Aquarius. Sincerity and a desire to serve others are also key influences. This is the time for you to detach emotionally from what does not serve you any more and let go of past hurts and regrets. Pragmatism and detachment are good qualities to exhibit during this time but also try to be imaginative and reinvent yourself if need be. Avoid convention and think right outside the box. Look to your future and assess what changes you need to make. The moonlight also shines on charitable causes. Avoid denying your feelings and becoming so eccentric you lose the support of others.

Moon in Pisces

Mysticism and dreaming are powerful influences when the moon is in Pisces. Compassion and empathy also come to the fore. It's the moment to focus on acknowledging, understanding and managing your feelings. It's also a great time to indulge your imagination and see where it takes you. Working on your intuitive ability during this time is key and it is also a time to focus on the meaning of the symbols that appear in your dreams at night. Avoid detaching yourself from reality and becoming too sensitive. Develop your creativity and intuition and meditate lots, but don't forget to also learn the importance and value of living in the real world.

Moon Power

There are many people who believe what the ancients believed – which modern science is now also proving – that the gravitational pull of the moon influences not just the tides but our moods, minds and bodies, too.

One area on which lunar cycles may have a great impact is fertility levels, with research indicating that more babies are born when the moon is full. Other preliminary studies show that the more a woman's cycles are coordinated with the moon's rhythms, the better her health and chances of getting pregnant. It seems that the new moon is the most fertile time for conception – perhaps because in the absence of moonlight, it is dark and therefore easier to fall asleep. A good night's sleep regulates hormones and your bodily rhythms and therefore enhances fertility.

In recent years, scientists have also become increasingly interested in the relationship between lunar cycles and sleep patterns. It has been shown that humans are more wakeful during full moons, when they have greater exposure to moonlight than during other lunar phases. So, if you are having difficulty sleeping, see which phase the moon is currently in and adjust accordingly. For example, when it's a full moon, you may want to make sure you wear an eye mask or use blackout blinds to minimize the energy-boosting lunar light and vibrations while you sleep. Alternatively, you could decide to use the extra illumination time to catch up on work, write in your journal or simply indulge yourself and bathe in the healing and empowering moonlight.

It's not just humans – even animals seem to sense the magic of moonlight. The full moon, for example, is a time when emotions tend to be heightened. If you've ever had a cat, dog or other pet, you may have noticed how they become more active when the moon is waxing or full. It often feels like there's a special energy when there's a full moon, and animals seem to sense that.

Through working with the moon, and understanding the energy shifts associated with each phase, you can manifest and celebrate your deepest wishes and dearest dreams. Find out how to follow the phases of the moon and different ways to harness lunar power in Chapter 2.

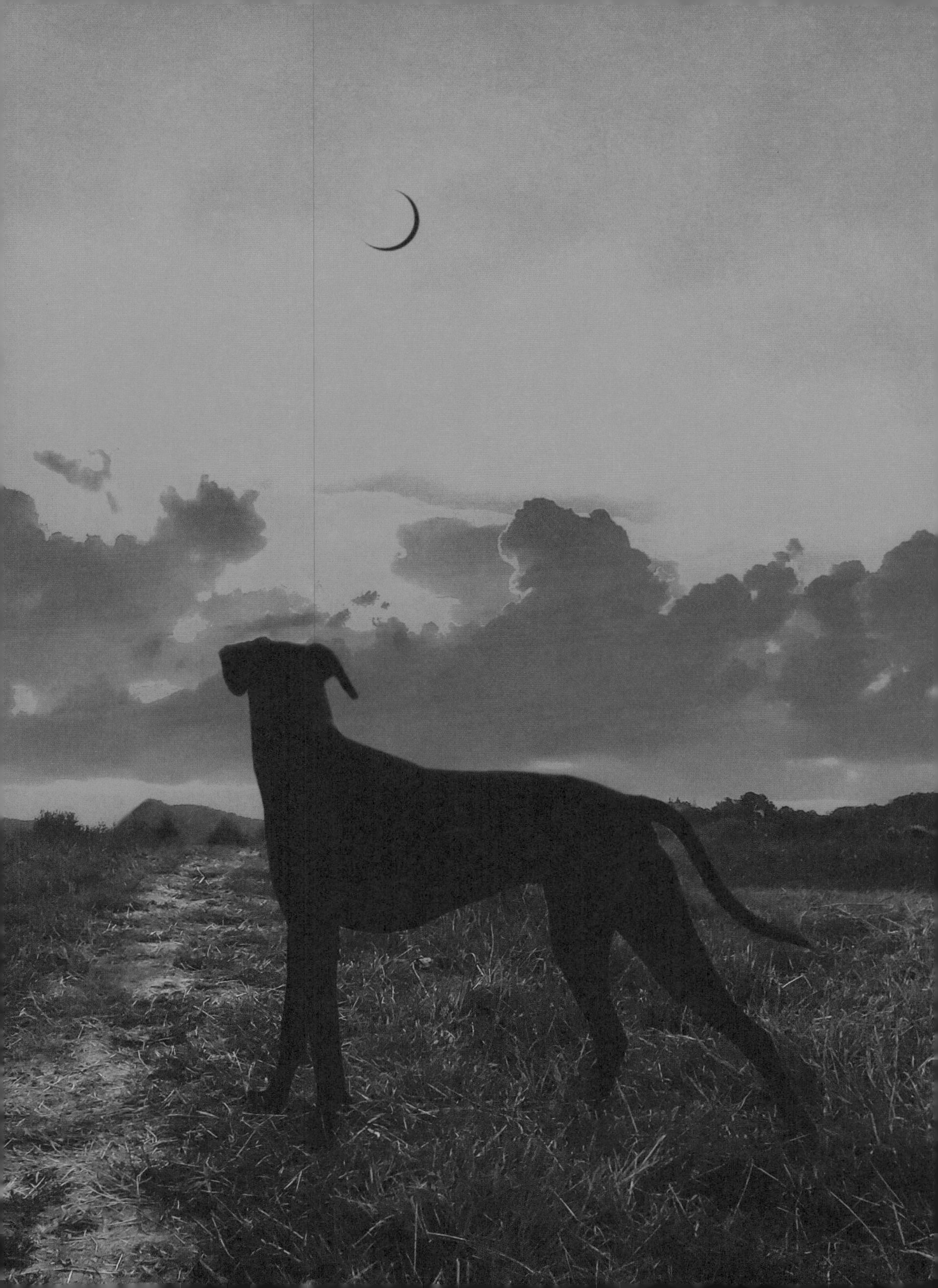

WORKING WITH THE MOON

Awareness of which phase the moon is currently in is vital for your moon work and, alongside that, you also need to know how to connect the moon to your deepest desires or intentions.

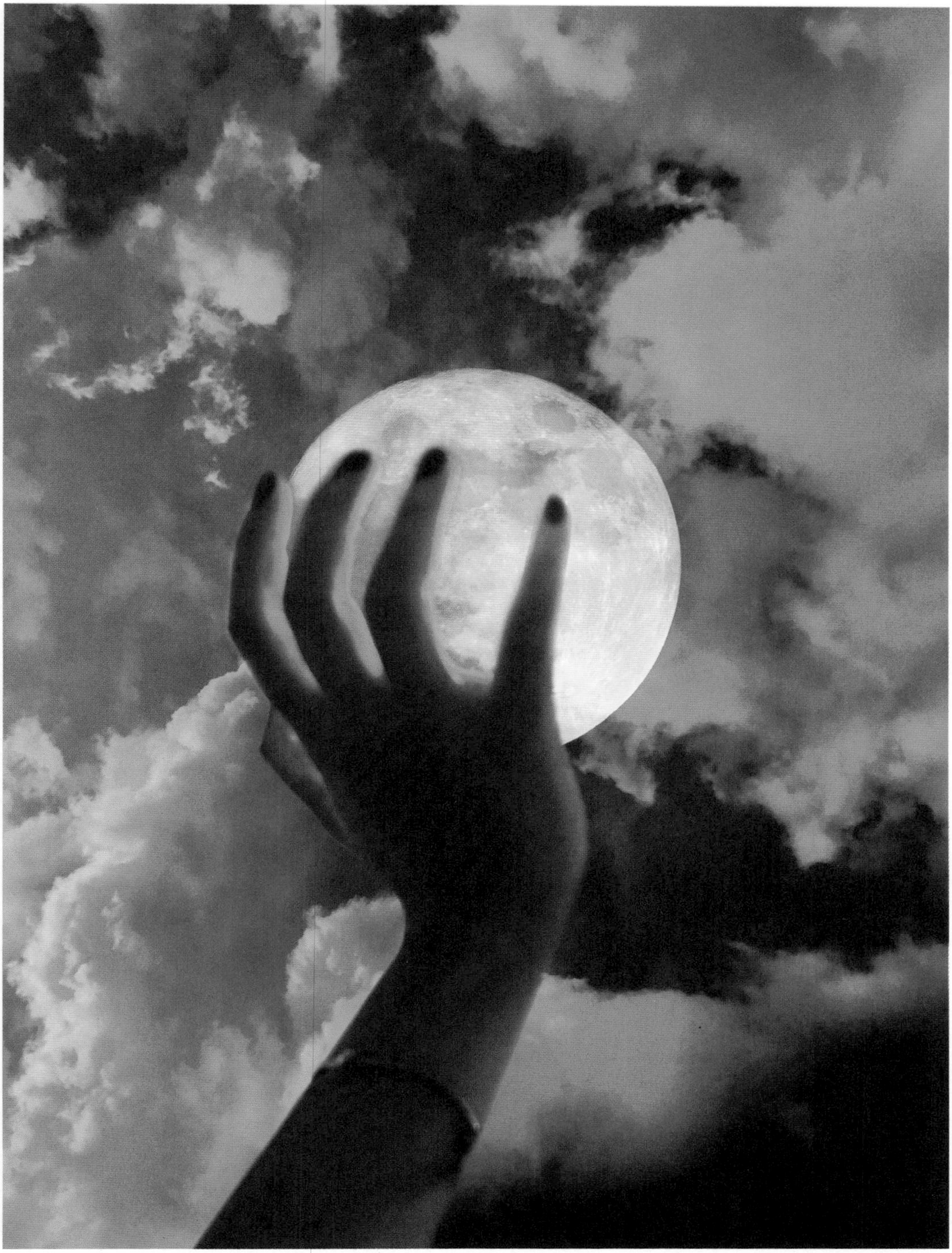

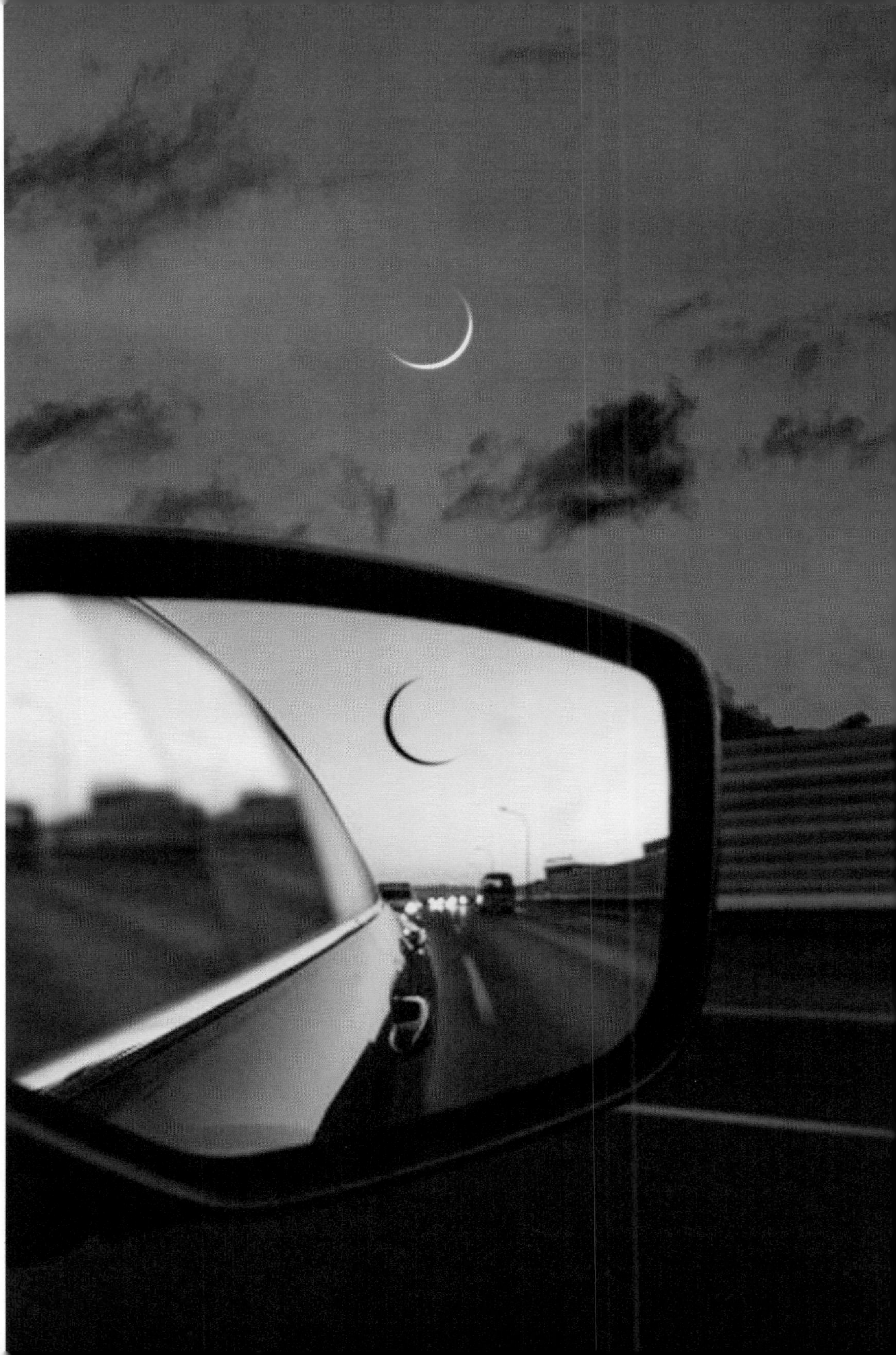

Following the Moon

The moon is one of the fastest moving celestial presences. When you start noticing and following her in the sky, you may at first find it a little hard to keep up with her constant transformations. No sooner has she eased into one phase than she is shifting forward to the next. Every 28 to 29 or so days, she moves from dark to new to full to hidden again and only spends a few days in each zodiac sign along the way. The moon is a traveller in the most magical sense of the word.

The moon's vital presence has much to teach us as she moves gracefully from one mysterious phase to the next. When the moon is dark, it is the ideal time to journey within. When there's a new moon, the moment is ideal for fresh starts and new beginnings, and when the moon is full, emotions and expectations run high. As the moon wanes, it's the moment to reflect, reassess and release what no longer serves you or is blocking you from moving forward. Tuning your emotions and energy in to the subtle changes in lunar vibrations during each phase can help you connect to your intuition so that you make better life choices. Making decisions about your life when the moon is most favourable for them to be successful can help you connect to the infinite potential within you, so you can manifest and celebrate your deepest desires.

Aligning the Moon to
Your Intentions

Intentions are your deepest desires or wishes. They may be a specific goal, for example losing weight, or they may be a desire for better health, a new job or attracting a loving long-term partner. Whatever your intentions are, you need to set them and be clear in your mind about what you want to manifest in your life before you ask the moon for her help.

I strongly urge you to spend time reflecting on what your deepest desires, life goals or priorities are before you start working with the moon in earnest. Write down those intentions, because committing things to paper sends a message to your mind that this is for real. The moon needs to know what you want to ask her for. And the more specific you are, the better.

You also need to be realistic in your goal setting. Asking the moon to help you win the lottery isn't realistic, as the odds are next to impossible, but asking the moon to help you find ways to increase your income is a more sensible intention. You also need to be disciplined and willing to do whatever it takes to manifest your intentions. Wishing under the moon will simply remain a wish. If you want good things to happen in your life, you need to take appropriate action to achieve your goals. Your moon awareness will help you tune in to your intuition so that it guides you towards making the best decisions about what actions to take. Passion and belief are other essential ingredients for success. You need to truly believe that your intentions can become real. When you work with the moon, you are always worthy of success.

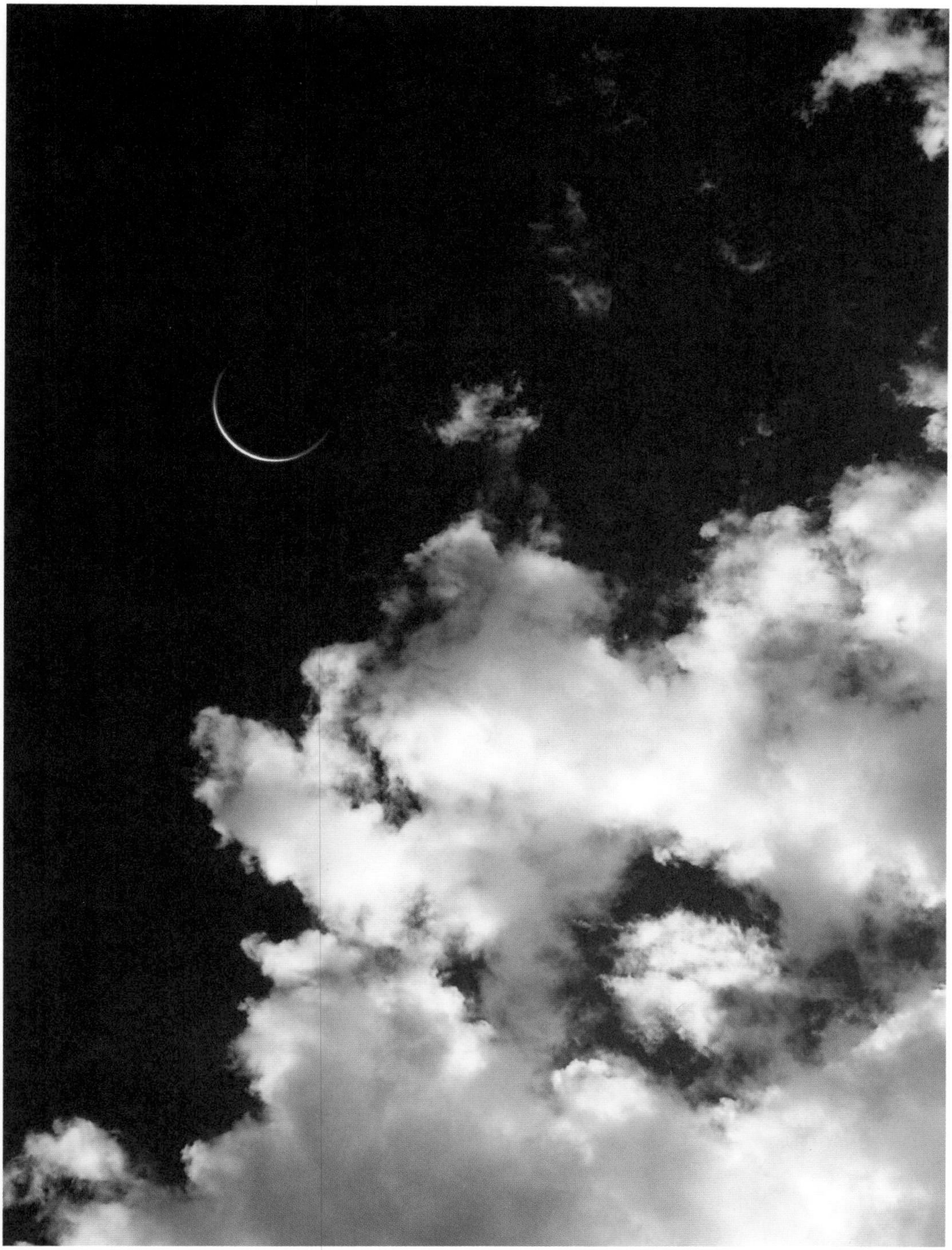

When and How to Work with the Moon

On page 36, you will find advice to help you align your intentions to the phases of the moon. You can further enhance your moon work by becoming aware of the zodiac sign that the moon is currently in so that you can modify your intentions according to the energies favoured by that sign (see pages 26–29).

It's also beneficial to bear in mind the day of the week on which you are working with the moon. Whether or not you are in tune with or interested in astrology, the specific day of the week that you pick to work with the moon is significant. Each day of the week has its own energy vibrations that can be used to give your lunar intentions another boost.

DAY OF THE WEEK	ALIGNED WITH	FOCUS
Monday	Moon	Spiritual development, healing, creativity
Tuesday	Mars	New projects, building confidence
Wednesday	Mercury	Communication, work issues
Thursday	Jupiter	Self-improvement, finances, travel
Friday	Venus	Self-care, relationships, love
Saturday	Saturn	Releasing negativity, assessing priorities
Sunday	Sun	Relaxation, holistic well-being

Each full moon has its own name and energy, too. There are various different names for the full moons, originating from different cultures. Below are some examples:

NORTHERN HEMISPHERE	SOUTHERN HEMISPHERE	NAME	ENERGY
January	July	Wolf Moon	Favours reflection
February	August	Snow Moon	Favours preparation
March	September	Worm Moon	Favours new beginnings
April	October	Pink Moon	Favours change
May	November	Flower Moon	Favours growth
June	December	Strawberry Moon	Favours harmony
July	January	Buck Moon	Favours relaxation
August	February	Sturgeon Moon	Favours preservation
September	March	Harvest Moon	Favours celebration
October	April	Hunter Moon	Favours release
November	May	Beaver Moon	Favours inner growth
December	June	Cold Moon	Favours giving

Making a Moon Journal

Writing down how you feel in a diary can help you better understand and manage your emotions and bring a sense of comfort and security. A moon journal is similar to a diary, although each day you make a note of the phase the moon is currently in and how you feel that phase is helping you move forward with your life. Your moon journal should focus not so much on events going on but on how you *feel* about yourself and the direction your life is taking. The better you understand yourself the more empowered you are likely to feel.

Lunar Preparations

Assuming your intentions are set and you are aware of the importance of aligning your goals with the phases of the moon, the scene is now set for your moon work to begin in earnest. In Chapter 3, you will find a series of moon fixes: rituals, spells, recipes and meditations you can perform. Location matters, and getting your moon fix outside, preferably at night, when the moon is in her element, is beneficial. You should always make sure you are in a safe, well-lit area. However, for many reasons being outdoors may not be possible: there are still many ways to align with the moon indoors or during the day.

When working indoors, it helps if you have a window that you can see the moon from but, if not, you can use a picture of the moon, which can also inspire. There are plenty of sumptuous pictures to choose from in this book. If you do decide to work with the moon outdoors, your garden can be a good place, as can a local park, beach or woods. Be aware that other people may find what you are doing unusual, so only go to local areas where you feel safe and protected.

Whether you are indoors or outdoors, aim to be alone. Before you begin, remove distractions. Shut off your phone. Sit quietly. Shake your hands to release any negativity. You may want to play relaxing music. A mini-visualization, in which you imagine your body surrounded by protective moonlight, or a mini-meditation, where you simply observe but don't engage with your thoughts and focus your attention on your breath, can also help bring moonlight into your mind. Do whatever feels right for you to set the scene.

Once you have completed your moon ritual, take as long as you need to readjust. If you are using candles, extinguish them and then do a big stretch to help you return to the present.

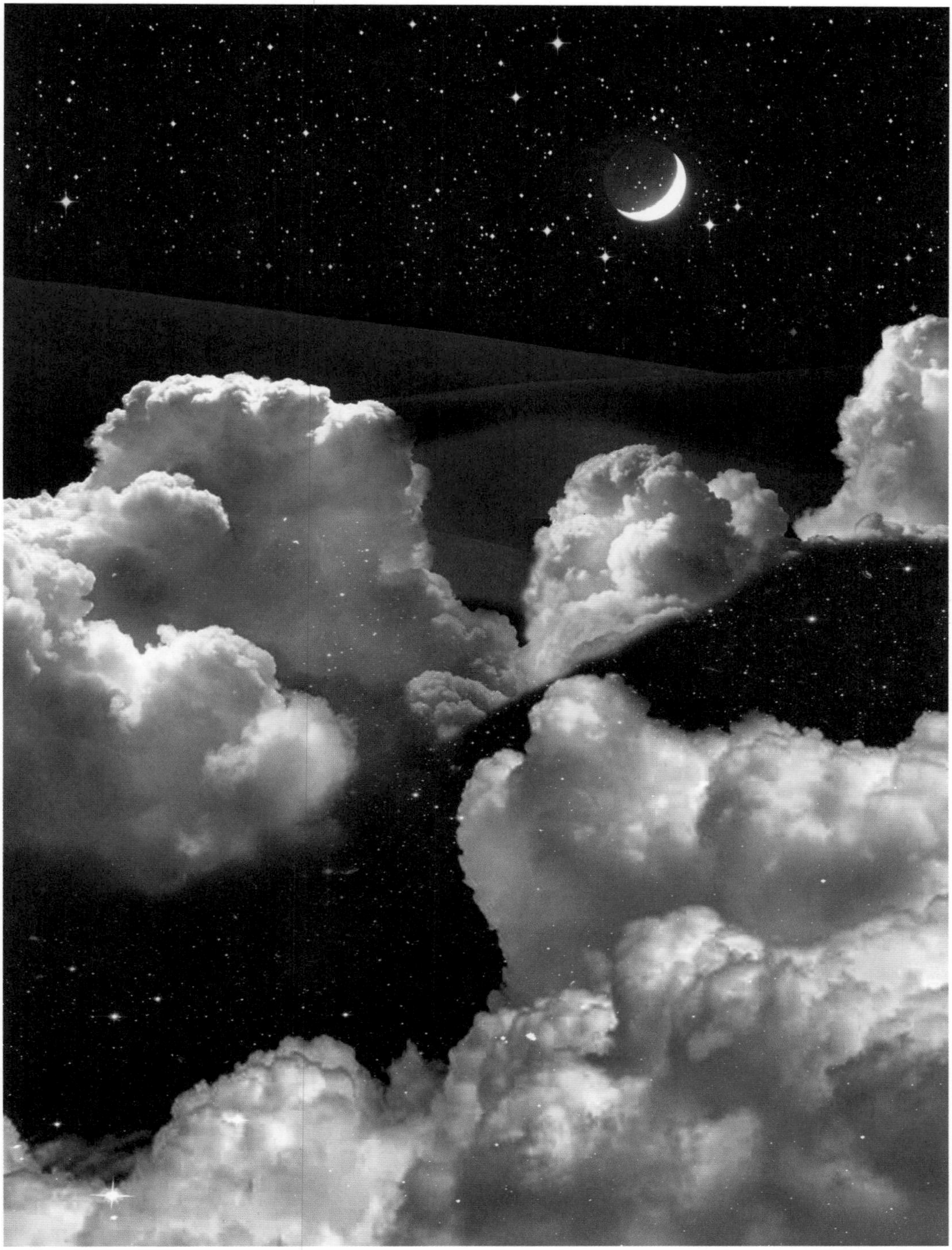

Moon Altar

A moon altar is a place to quietly reflect, meditate, pray to the moon, set your intentions and hear the moon's answers. It is also the place to store any items you may choose to use to enhance your moon work. Creating a moon altar is highly recommended for when you perform your moon fixes, but it is not essential.

Make Your Altar

Your moon altar doesn't have to be anything complicated. Here are a few ideas for what to use:

- Decorate a cardboard box – a great benefit of this is that it is portable, and also offers space to store your tools.
- A small table, a bookshelf or a corner of the room will also suffice if you want a permanent location.
- Build and carve your own altar out of wood or other natural materials. Avoid metal and plastic as much as possible.

Place Your Altar

Placing your altar to face a certain direction will enhance your moon work by tuning in to the vibrations of that direction.

DIRECTION	ELEMENT	USE FOR
North	Earth	Health, healing, communicating with spiritual powers
East	Air	New beginnings
South	Fire	Love, relationships
West	Water	Forgiveness, letting go, self-confidence

Lunar Crystals

Just like lunar power, crystals run on energy vibrations and each one has its own unique energy frequency, which can be used to help restore balance to all aspects of your life by interacting with your own energy, naturally absorbing it or directing it. So, the vibration of a specific crystal, when used in a moon ritual, can help focus lunar power more clearly on your intentions.

There are many wonderful healing crystals you can use in your moon work. You don't need to buy huge stones and can use small inexpensive ones obtained online or from gift shops. Before you pick a stone to use in your moon work, make sure that you enjoy looking at it and that it feels good when you hold it.

The crystals listed below are particularly excellent for moon work:

- **MOONSTONE**: igniting intuition
- **ROSE QUARTZ**: attracting love
- **CLEAR QUARTZ**: achieving holistic balance
- **AMETHYST**: boosting concentration
- **ANGELITE**: enhancing spiritual awareness
- **OPAL**: boosting health
- **CARNELIAN**: increasing desire and drive
- **GARNET**: easing emotional pain
- **MALACHITE**: increasing energy
- **PERIDOT**: boosting success
- **JADE**: attracting abundance
- **SELENITE**: connecting to inner wisdom
- **LAPIS LAZULI**: healing
- **AQUAMARINE**: easing stress
- **TURQUOISE**: protecting from negativity
- **LABRADORITE**: enhancing inner strength

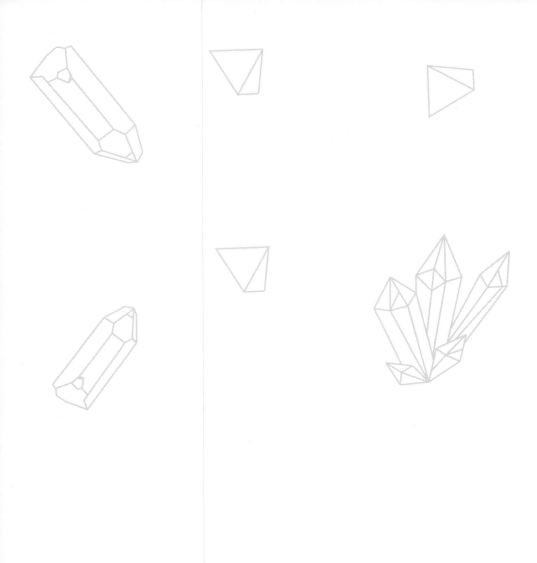

If you are uncertain which crystals are best to use in a moon fix, you can't go wrong with moonstone, rose quartz or clear quartz.

Charging Your Crystals

Before using the crystals, you need to 'charge' them. Leave them overnight under the light of the moon, either outside or on a windowsill. You can charge your crystals during any of the moon's phases, but the most potent time is during the waxing moon phase when energy is increasing. Once you have charged your chosen crystal by moonlight, you then need to turbo-charge it with your intentions by holding it in your hand and visualizing whatever it is that you want to manifest in your life.

Candles, Incense, Herbs and Oils

Using candles, healing herbs and essential oils can enhance all your moon rituals. They are not essential but are useful tools that can help get you into a mystical state of mind.

Candles

If you light a candle before performing a ritual, do not leave them unattended; keep them away from flammable materials, children and pets; and extinguish them safely afterwards. Candles symbolize the gift of light and clear sight in the darkness. The candle itself represents life on earth, and the flame spiritual or psychic potential. The colour of the candle is significant because colours carry their own energy vibrations, but if you don't have any coloured ones, white is perfect for moon rituals because it is the colour of healing, peace and pure potential. Here are the energies associated with various colours:

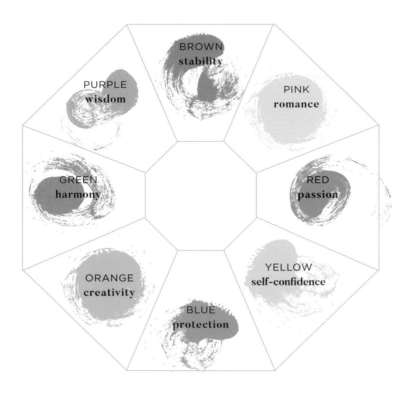

BROWN
stability

PINK
romance

PURPLE
wisdom

RED
passion

GREEN
harmony

YELLOW
self-confidence

ORANGE
creativity

BLUE
protection

Incense and Herbs

Burning incense when you perform a ritual can add to the sacred ambience, but it is important that you choose a scent that you find appealing. Here are some recommended herbs and scents for moon work and their common uses, but be sure to find what works best for you. Check with your doctor that there will be no contraindications if using herbs in your diet.

- **LOVE AND RELATIONSHIPS**: rose, thyme, musk, apple, cinnamon, vanilla, jasmine
- **HEALTH**: sage, rosemary, lavender, lemon grass, juniper, pine, ginger
- **SPIRITUALITY**: sage, rose, sweetgrass, violet, frankincense, jasmine, pine
- **SUCCESS**: vanilla, almond, juniper, sage, peppermint, orange, allspice
- **SELF-CONFIDENCE**: chamomile, peppermint, lemon balm, jasmine
- **CONCENTRATION**: peppermint, orange, rosemary, lemon balm, eyebright

Essential Oils

There are certain essential oils that correspond well with each moon phase. You can place a few drops of essential oil in a ritual bath or diffuse or spray it on your clothes or pillow. Essential oils can influence both your mind and your emotions and, when charged with lunar power, they can be even more therapeutic. Below are some suggested scents to get you started. Experiment, though, to find the right oil to match each lunar phase for you. If you are new to using oils, seek expert advice on safe ways to use them before experimenting.

- **NEW MOON**: ginger and pine
- **WAXING MOON**: lavender and vanilla
- **FULL MOON**: rose and jasmine
- **WANING MOON**: eyebright and rosemary

Bathing in the Moonlight

Moon bathing is incredibly healing and balancing for body and mind and it is especially beneficial if you are feeling run-down physically, mentally or emotionally. The ideal time to do this is when the moon is full or new. Then, her healing potential is at its height and her cleansing potential is at its peak. This can be done either outdoors in a safe environment, or indoors, as long as you can see the moon.

YOU WILL NEED
- Moonlight
- 20–30 minutes

METHOD
1. Wear as few clothes as possible. Bathing nude is recommended in the comfort of your own home, but only if you feel comfortable and it is safe to do so.
2. Shake your hands and feet to release any negativity.
3. While standing, stretch your arms up in the air and your feet to the tips of your toes. Reach for the moon and the stars with your stretch. If you prefer to do this ritual sitting down, straighten your spine and look up at the moon.
4. Then, sit or, better still, lie down somewhere comfortable and close your eyes and relax.
5. Take some slow, deep breaths and let the cooling, calming light of the moon shower down on you and soothe your body, mind and heart.
6. Visualize silver, blue and white light flowing into you and surrounding you.
7. Simply lie or sit there soaking in the illumination of the moon for 20–30 minutes. Feel yourself filling up with her love and lunar power.

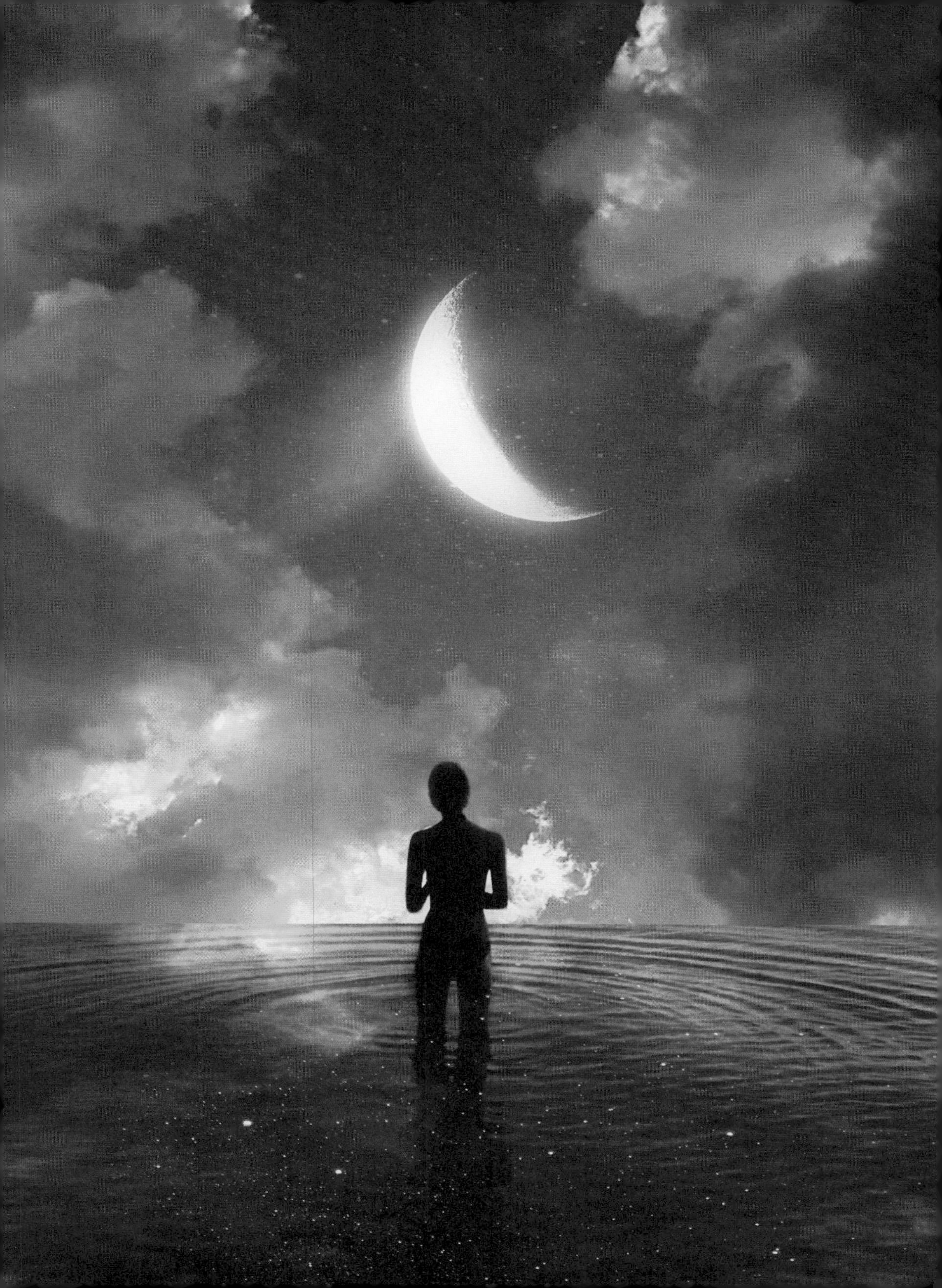

CHAPTER 3

YOUR MOON FIX

This chapter will help you find practical solutions to modern-life problems. Each subsection is arranged around a particular theme and offers lunar advice and a series of spells, rituals, meditations and recipes to help with a particular need.

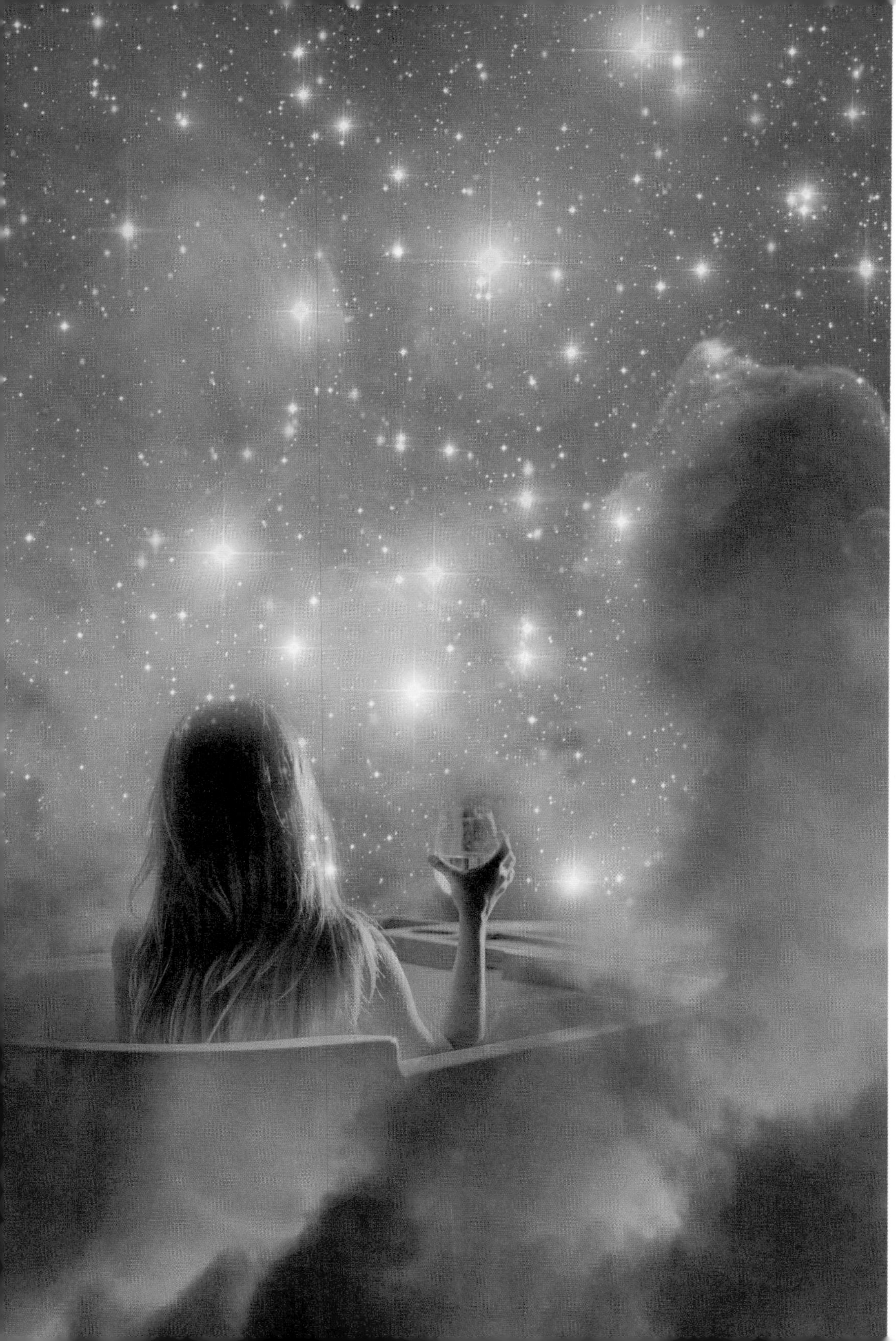

JOY AND SUCCESS

Since ancient times, lunar deities have been strongly associated with fertility, good fortune and pleasure. To this day, the popular motivational phrase 'shooting for the moon' is linked to the search for success in life. You will find moon fixes here to help you attract happiness and to prosper. There are also fixes to boost your self-esteem, ignite your motivation and increase your chances of success. Every fix will help you achieve a direct, personal relationship with the moon, so that joyful interaction with her starts to feel completely spontaneous.

> **FOR BEST RESULTS** Perform this ritual daily for at least a month as that's one lunar cycle. The more you do it, the easier it will become for you to connect to the moon's energy.

Ritual for Happiness

Moon energy connects directly to your intuition – the wise and loving part of you that can guide you towards what is joyful and away from what is draining. The problem is most of us are so busy and distracted these days, especially by the constant demands of our mobiles, we can't hear the voice of our intuition clearly. This moon fix to refocus you towards contentment will only take a few minutes and you don't even need to see the moon or wait until nightfall. You can do it at any time of day that suits you.

YOU WILL NEED
- Picture of the moon
- Your phone switched off or to silent

METHOD
1 Go somewhere quiet where you won't be distracted.
2 Sit down, close your eyes, take a few deep breaths and then visualize the moon. You can imagine it in any of its glorious phases; it doesn't have to be the phase it is currently in. See, in your mind's eye, the moon you love the most.
3 Silently 'talk' to the moon with your thoughts and feelings. It doesn't matter what you think or feel. With your heart and mind 'tell' the moon you welcome any interaction and value her guidance and wisdom.
4 When you are ready, tell the moon that you will be talking to her again tomorrow. Open your eyes, take a deep, energizing breath and smile as broadly as you can. As you smile, feel the energy, power and pure joy of the moon's illumination rising within you.

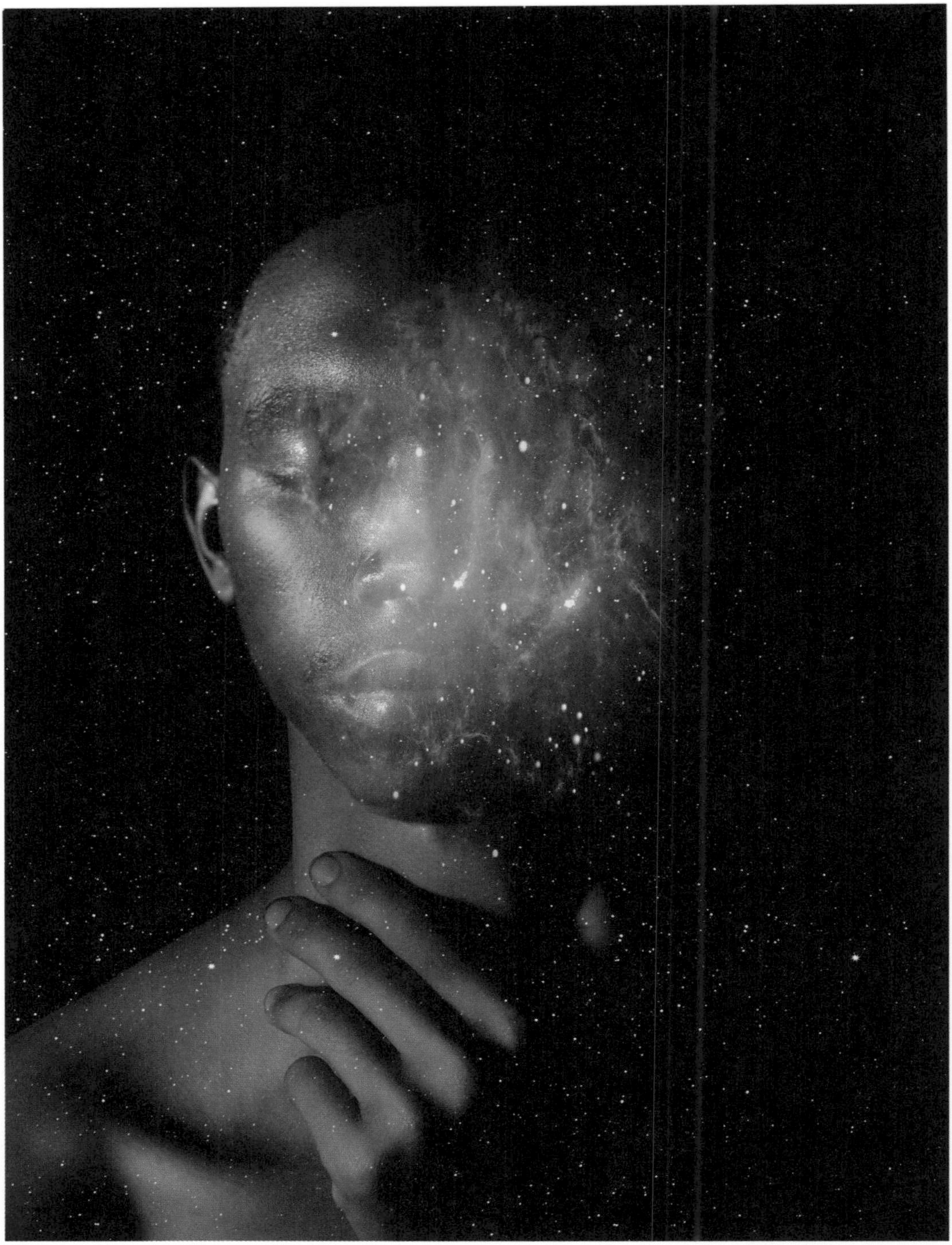

FOR BEST RESULTS You can perform this ritual during any moon phase but the optimum time is when the moon is waning, as this phase favours releasing and letting go.

Attract Abundance

Tuning in to lunar power can help you identify your unconscious abundance blocks – those limiting beliefs you have that prevent the flow of abundance connecting to you. These blocks are usually the result of inherited beliefs, social expectations or personal traumas and they make us feel that we are not in control of our lives. Surrender these blocks to the moon's energy and trust her to purge them from your mind and clear the way for abundance to flow effortlessly into your life.

YOU WILL NEED
- Pencil or pen
- Piece of blank paper

METHOD
1 Sketch the moon by hand on a piece of paper. It needn't be precise and it doesn't matter which phase you draw the moon in or how well you can draw, just draw a moon shape that speaks to you.
2 Focus your attention on that shape and then write down one reason why you feel you haven't got enough money or why you don't feel wealthy. How do you really feel about money? Do not censor or sense check anything, just write.
3 Read what you have written. Imagine moonlight shining down on you and say out loud once, 'I surrender this limiting and dark belief to the clarifying light of the moon.'
4 Ask the moon to help you release this abundance block and to give you whatever you need to feel you are worthy of abundance.
5 Close this ritual by thanking the moon and tearing up or burning the piece of paper. Repeat this ritual as often as necessary to help banish those abundance blocks.

MOONSTONE Available in white, grey, yellow, blue, green, silver and black, the moonstone has been used for thousands of years as an amulet of good luck, healing, harmony and protection.

Invite Good Luck

Create your own good luck charm infused with the energy and power of the moon. Carry the light and inspiring energy of your crystal with you at all times, either on your person, in your car or whenever you need to travel. If you prefer not to carry it around with you, place it on your moon altar or somewhere special to you and imprint the image of the crystal on your mind so you can visualize it physically whenever you need inspiration.

YOU WILL NEED

- Moonstone crystal

METHOD

1. Hold your moonstone crystal tightly with it cupped in your palm; place your hand on your heart.
2. Say out loud or in your mind, 'With great love and joy I greet you, beloved stone of the moon. All success, all good fortune is mine.' Alternatively, if you don't want to use those words, simply ask your crystal to help you connect to the protective energies of the moon wherever you are.
3. Then, give thanks for all the good fortune in your life.
4. Your crystal is now personalized for your own use and the next step is to charge it under the light of the moon (see page 45).
5. Once charged by the moon, be sure to spend a few moments each day by yourself reconnecting with your crystal. Hold it in your hands or visualize it and give thanks to the moon for all that you have to be grateful for in your life.

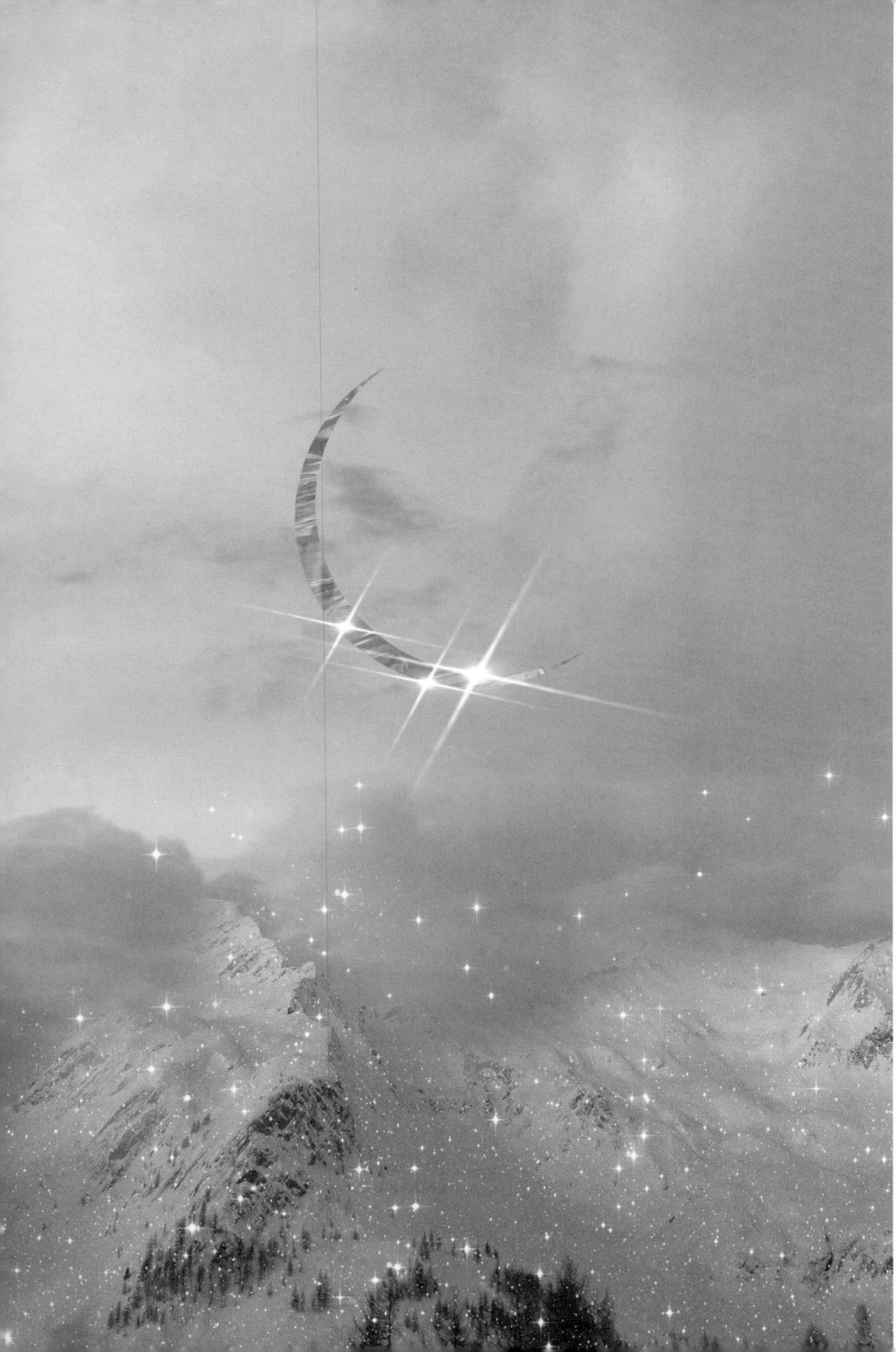

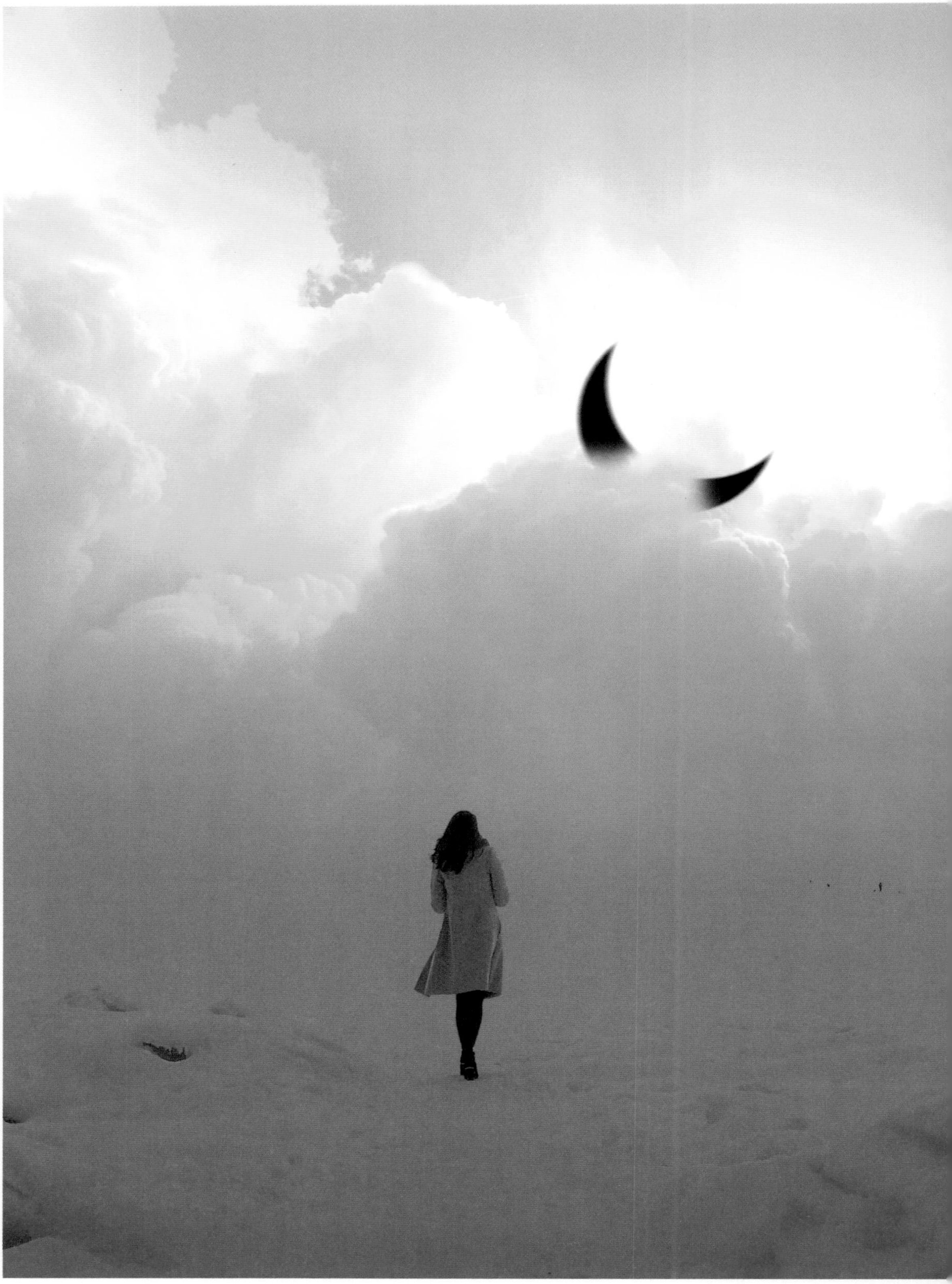

FOR BEST RESULTS Adapting the spell to the phases of the moon will connect you on a deeper and more intimate level.

Spell for Empowerment

The goddess moon was believed to be the empowered queen of the night sky. This simple lunar spell will help boost your feelings of self-esteem because if that is low, happiness will elude you. Repeat throughout the lunar cycle and give it your full attention. The power of spells comes from the intention behind them, so focus and make it clear what you are asking for.

YOU WILL NEED

- Smartphone
- Photograph of the moon
- Moon altar
- White candle
- Matches/lighter
- Moonstone, or alternative crystal (see page 44)

METHOD

1 Take a photo of the moon and place that photo on your moon altar. If you can't see the moon, research which phase it is in and use a photo you find online or draw that phase on a piece of paper instead.

2 Light a white candle and place your crystal in front of the photo. Now spend a few moments looking at your photo. Then, say the following – or choose your own words according to whichever phase the moon is in:

- **NEW MOON**: 'Thank you, new moon, for awakening my self-belief.'
- **WAXING MOON**: 'Thank you, waxing moon, for building my self-worth.'
- **FULL MOON**: 'Thank you, full moon, for giving me all the personal empowerment I need.'
- **WANING MOON**: 'Thank you, waning moon, for releasing all my shyness and fears.'

3 Savour the moment. Believe that the moon will bless you with feelings of empowerment. Then gently blow out the candle.

FOR BEST RESULTS If you align your goals to the energies of each lunar phase, this combination of the power of intention aligned with lunar power is potent.

Motivation Ritual

Writing down your goals under the light of the moon can inspire and empower your life. Your thoughts need managing and motivating on a daily basis so that they work for you and not against you. What you focus your attention and energy on is what you are most likely to draw into your life. This moon fix encourages you to make the best use of the moon's powerful lunar energy shifts by adapting your intentions and daily goal setting.

YOU WILL NEED

- Pen or pencil
- Paper
- Your intention

METHOD

1 Every night before you go to bed, glance at the moon to see what phase it is in or if you can't see it, find out what phase it is in.

2 Write down your goals or what you want to focus your attention on the following day, adapting those intentions to the current phase of the moon as follows:
   - **NEW MOON**: Goal setting should focus on planning when the moon is dark and unseen in the sky, then new beginnings when she begins to emerge. This may include starting something that you have never done before or doing things you already do in a new or different way. Start a new hobby, begin that novel, travel to work a different way.
   - **WAXING MOON**: Write down goals that focus on following through and building momentum. This is the ideal time to consolidate and work on what you have already started. It's also the time for patience – for example, keep working on that assignment, do those chores you have been avoiding.

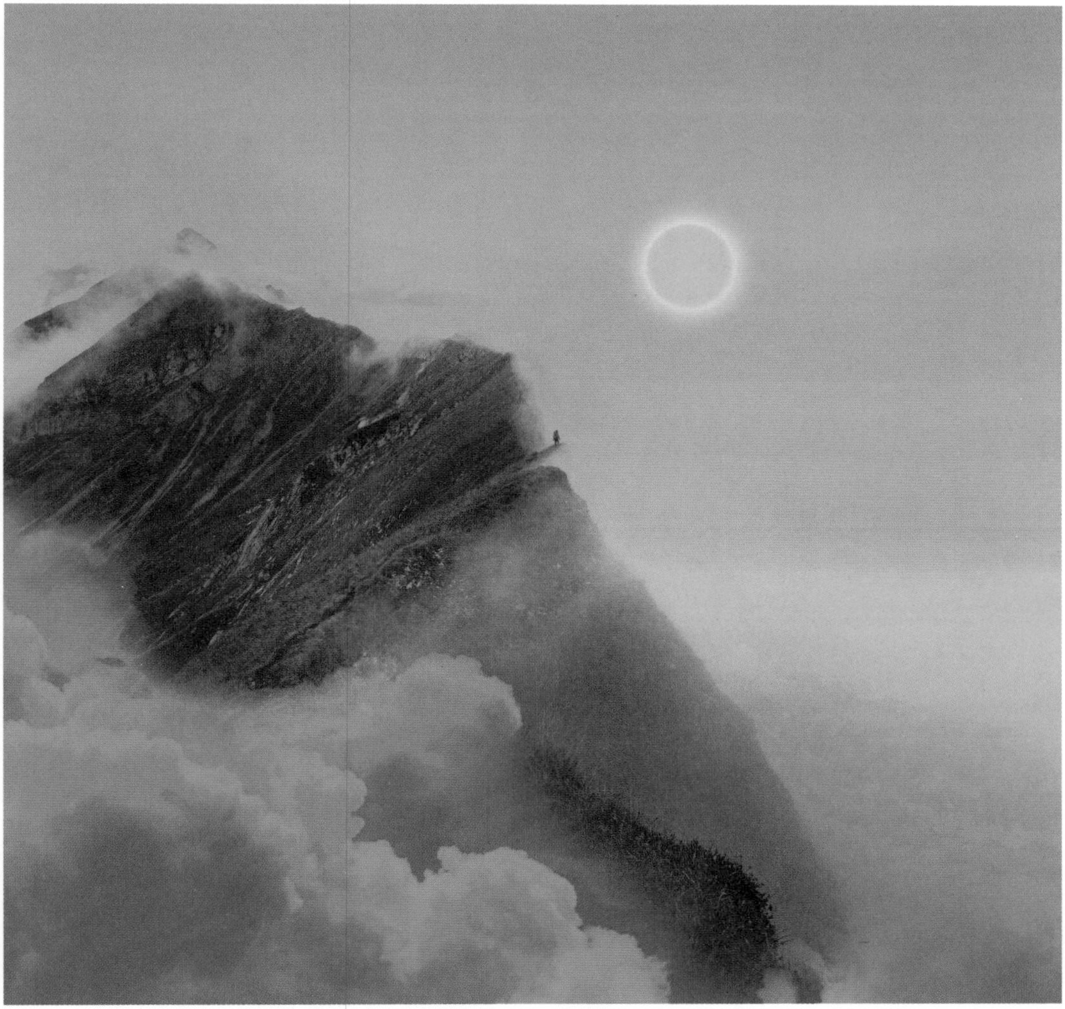

- **FULL MOON**: Write down goals that focus on self-care. Find ways to celebrate your achievements and monitor your progress. This is also the ideal time to tidy up all areas of your life so you can let go of what is no longer needed or is holding you back.
- **WANING MOON**: Focus your goal setting during this phase on rest, rejuvenation and supporting the well-being of others, as well as your own. It's also the ideal time for gratitude and for delegating or leaving behind what doesn't serve you any more. Make sure your goals align with your values and what really matters in your life.

> **MANTRAS** These are high-energy words/phrases that raise our energy vibrations.

Mantras for Optimism

To attract what we want into our lives, we truly have to believe we deserve it. We need an optimistic mindset. Use the energetic power of a moon mantra to draw down some of the moon's shining light towards you, so that looking on the bright side of things comes naturally.

YOU WILL NEED
- Mantra
- The sound of your own voice

METHOD
1. Think of your mantra as your daily personal prayer to the moon. The ideal time to say it is when you see the moon in the night sky from your window or, better still, when standing outside.
2. If you can't see the moon clearly, choose a picture in this book and visualize it in the sky.
3. It doesn't matter what phase the moon is for this moon fix. You are simply raising your vibration to meet the moon through your mantra. You need to say your moon mantra out loud to hear what you are saying.
4. You can create your own mantra, but something along these lines is perfect: 'When I open myself to the light of the moon, I attract everything that is good.'
5. Alternatively, you may simply want to chant the word 'moon' and repeat it over and over again for around a minute. Whenever you say your moon mantra feel the light energy and optimism of the moon flowing towards you.
6. Begin to notice when others say the word 'moon' in your daily life and how this makes you feel. It will likely send shivers down your spine.

> **FENG SHUI** This teaches you how to balance and harmonize the energies in your chosen space to increase your chances of attracting wealth, joy and success.

Planting for Prosperity

The new moon is when the moon's energy is increasing with each passing day and it is the ideal time to practise some feng shui prosperity-building techniques. According to feng shui experts, vibrant green indoor plants are believed to attract prosperity, with money plants in particular thought to enhance the flow of energy. Planting seeds or purchasing green plants when the moon is new and waxing and placing them on your windowsill can help attract wealth and a positive flow of energy into your life.

YOU WILL NEED
- Small money plant or any vibrant green indoor plant of your choice
- Windowsill
- Water

METHOD
1 When the moon is dark or new, purchase a small green pot plant.
2 To attract the energy of wealth and abundance, place it on a windowsill with plenty of light in your home or work area – do not put it in your bedroom or bathroom.
3 Water and feed your prosperity plant as needed.
4 Every time you care for or notice your plant, ask the moon to bring good things into your life.

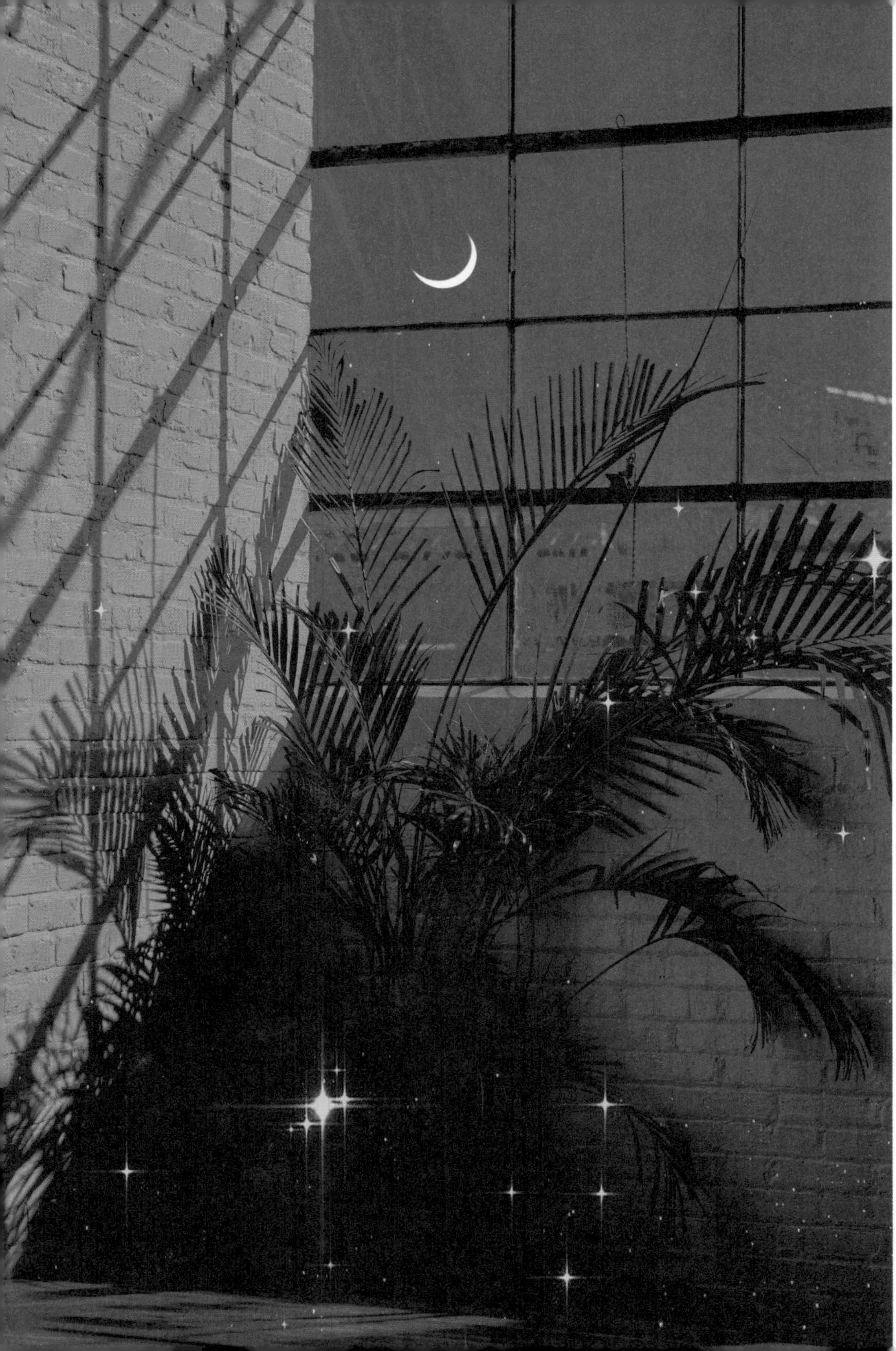

Recipes for Success

This moon fix encourages you to cook and eat at least one of your meals each day with the moon and its current phase in mind. Choosing food that resonates with the natural phases of the moon can bring balance to your mental well-being and, by so doing, dramatically increase your chances of happiness and success. Being more physically in tune with the moon makes it easier for your thoughts, feelings and actions to tap in to the lunar power.

- The new moon is a time for keeping your food choices light. Salads should reign supreme and you need to make sure you get plenty of fluids.
- The waxing moon is when a diet rich in energy-boosting fish, chicken, beans, legumes and vegetables is best. Don't forget to stock up on herbs and spices, too.
- The full moon is the time to indulge in richer and more extravagant cuisine.
- And the waning moon turns the spotlight on cleansing, wholesome nurturing foods, such as rice and soup.

See opposite for a delicious full-moon treat to get you thinking along the right lines.

SWEET TREATS Chocolate not only tastes heavenly, it is rich in powerful nutrients that are beneficial to your health.

Full Moon Hot Chocolate

There is no better way to treat yourself than with a delicious mug of homemade hot chocolate when there's a full moon. In moderation, it's the perfect treat for moon lovers.

INGREDIENTS

- 150 ml/5 fl oz/⅔ cup full or skimmed/nonfat milk/soya milk
- Pinch of sugar
- 25–30 g/1 oz chopped chocolate
- Mini marshmallows, whipped cream, chocolate sprinkles, to serve

METHOD

1 Pour the milk into a pan. Add a pinch of sugar. Stir with a wooden spoon over a medium heat, until tiny bubbles start to surface on the milk at the sides of the pan. Do not bring it to boil.
2 Add the chopped chocolate to the heated milk and stir until fully melted and creamy.
3 Serve in your favourite mug topped with mini marshmallows, whipped cream and chocolate sprinkles.

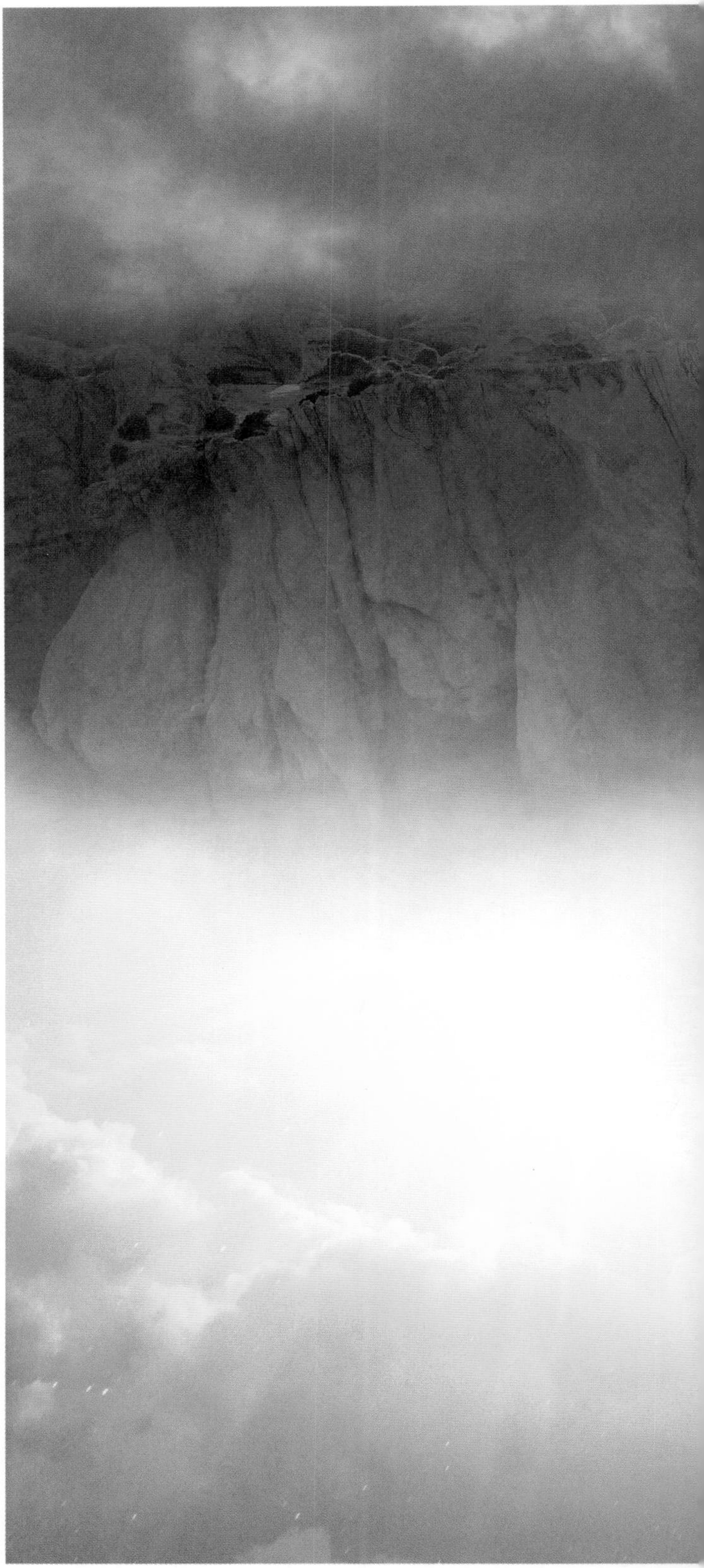

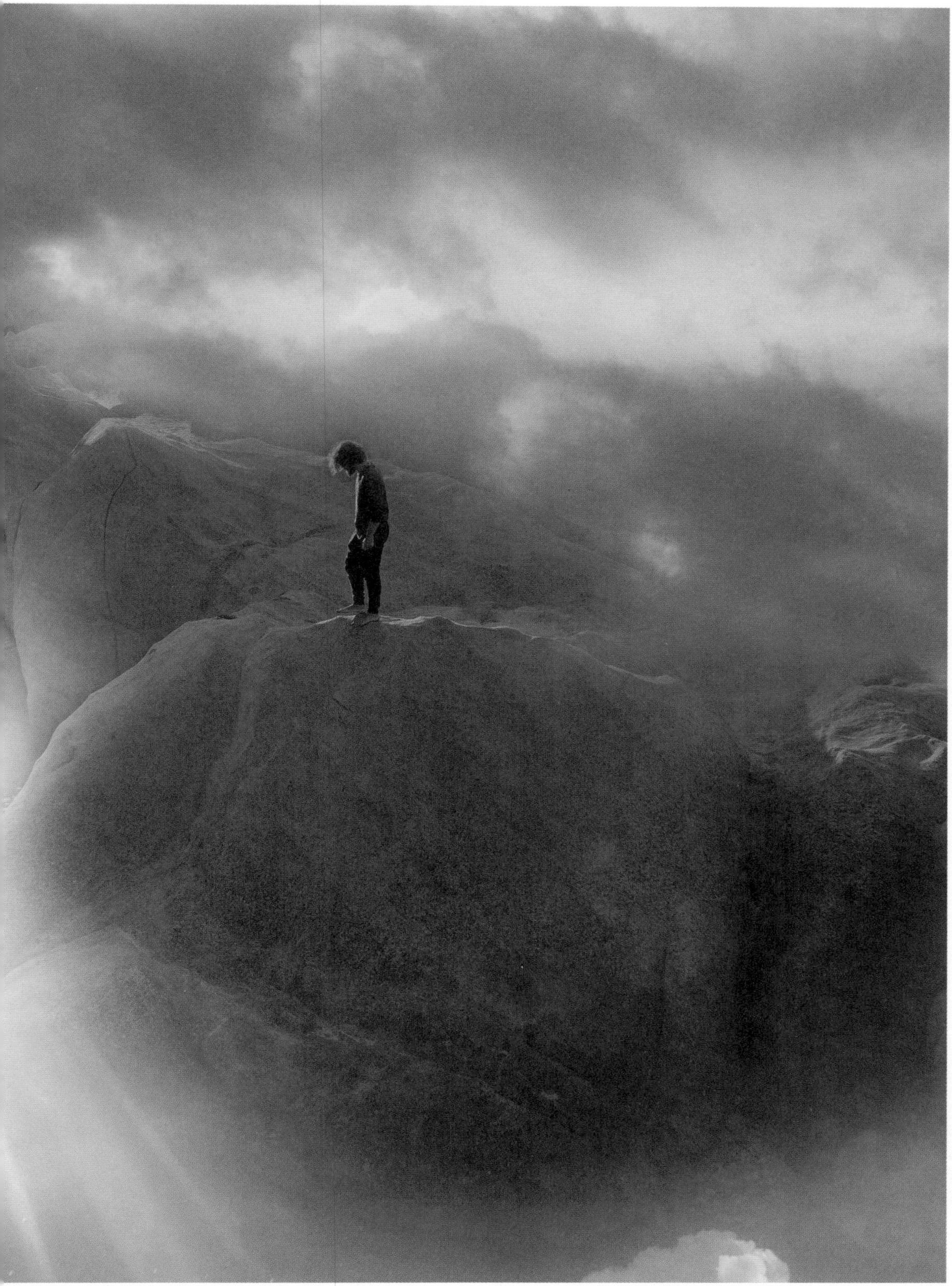

LOVE AND RELATIONSHIPS

As the closest celestial body to planet earth, the moon returns nightly to us like a loyal and loving companion. She symbolizes female energy, fertility and the relationship between a mother and her children. The moon fixes you will discover in this section are all designed to help you attract love and manage your emotions so that you can see your relationship to yourself and to others more clearly. Physical action is also crucial in order to attract love. Perform these fixes to find your soulmate, ignite passion and improve all your relationships, in particular the most important one of all – the relationship you have with yourself.

FOR BEST RESULTS Friday and Sunday are optimum days to practise this ritual.

Grow Self-Love

This ritual shines the moonlight on the relationship you have with yourself. You can't give to others what you don't have yourself. Connecting to lunar energy naturally enhances your compassion and empathy. Both qualities are important for successful relationships, but offering your compassion and empathy without a firm grounding in self-love can result in toxic, unbalanced relationships in which you do all the giving and others do all the taking. Harnessing the energies of the moon to increase self-love can therefore bring harmony and balance to *all* your relationships.

YOU WILL NEED
- Rose quartz crystal
- Your heart
- Your hand

METHOD
1. Sit somewhere quiet and place your rose quartz crystal nearby.
2. Close your eyes, breathe deeply and gradually focus all your attention on your heart beating inside you.
3. Think about the things and people you love and imagine that you are breathing not from your lungs but from your heart.
4. Visualize the moon forming a heart shape in the sky. Imagine that heart-shaped moon beating in time with your own heart.
5. Then, keeping that image of loving connection between your heart and the moon in your mind's eye, place your hand on your heart, sit up straight and say out loud the following affirmation, depending on the phase of the moon:
   - **WAXING MOON**: 'I am worthy of love.'
   - **WANING MOON**: 'I am grateful for all that I am.'
   Saying the words out loud is important. You need to hear yourself say them – and the moon needs to hear you say them, too.
6. Thank the moon for her loving illumination and slowly open your eyes.

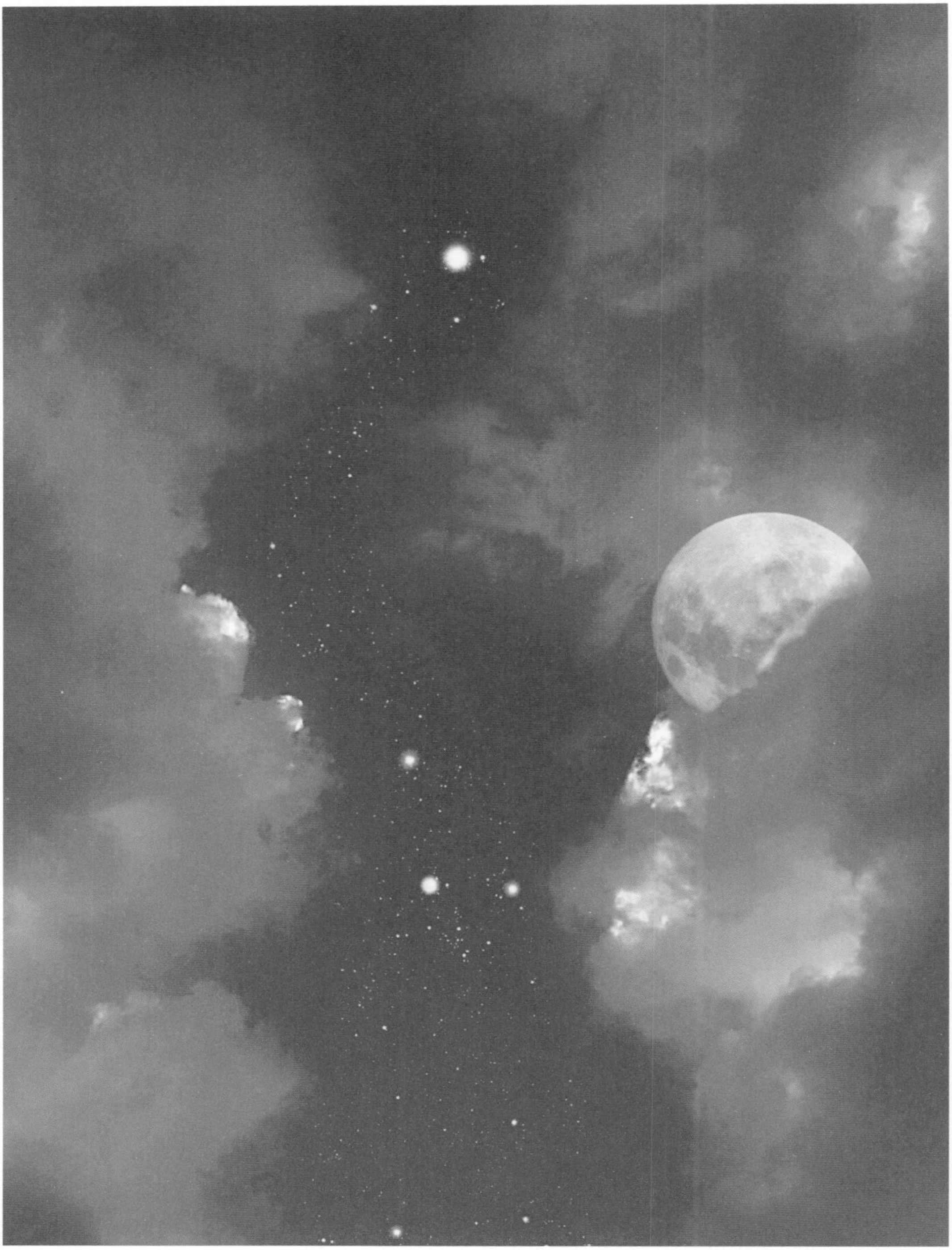

FOR BEST RESULTS
Sunday is an especially healing
day to perform this.

Find Forgiveness

Forgiveness is one of the most important ingredients in successful relationships.
Bitterness and anger block the loving energy of the moon. Sometimes the
person we need to forgive the most is ourself, so this ritual can also be used
for that purpose. This moon fix should be performed during the new moon.
It is the optimum time for fresh starts and nothing gives a relationship a more
positive start than forgiveness.

YOU WILL NEED
- Clear quartz crystal
- Piece of blank paper, preferably letter paper
- Pen
- Envelope

METHOD
1   It is beneficial to place a calming clear quartz crystal nearby.
2   Find a piece of paper, pen and envelope. Formal letter-writing paper
    would be ideal.
3   Write a short letter to someone who has upset or hurt you. It can be
    anyone in your present life or from your past, and the person could be
    alive or in spirit.
4   As you write, connect with loving compassion to that person and
    understand that it is only human for people to hurt other people. Remind
    yourself that forgiving is not the same as forgetting. You are simply
    releasing feelings of bitterness that have weighed down your heart.
    Then, put your letter in the envelope and go outside.
5   Under the light of the new moon say that person's name out loud and
    tear up or burn the letter. It is now time for you to move forward and
    open your heart so love and peace can replace bitterness.
6   Once you have finished, be sure to remain true to its spirit throughout
    the entire lunar cycle. If it is not yet new moon, send loving thoughts
    and feelings to someone you need to forgive. Then, when the new moon
    arrives, perform the ritual.

FOR BEST RESULTS This moon fix should be performed at full moon when her power is at its height. There can be no better time to trust yourself and your ability to attract positive and loving relationships into your life. Monday is a beneficial day to perform this ritual.

Build Trust

Trust is one of the most important things in any relationship. It can take years to build and a moment to break. This moon fix is one that can help you rebuild trust in yourself, others and even the universe itself. The moon is our most loyal and trusted companion. The more we tune in to her faithful lunar power, the more we can grow those trusting qualities within ourselves, and attract relationships that are lasting and loyal.

YOU WILL NEED

- White candle
- Matches/lighter
- Turquoise crystal
- Prayer

METHOD

1. When the moon is full, light a white candle. White is the colour of cleansing and protection. It inspires trust and hope.
2. Place a turquoise crystal nearby.
3. Sit quietly beside your candle and watch it glow. Then say out loud a prayer to the full moon, along these lines:

   Loyal and loving Moon, you are a constant illumination in my life. You shine bright and then you retreat every month but, now that you are at the height of your power, I ask you to attract loving and loyal relationships into my life. Thank you for ensuring that I am not alone. Thank you for always watching over me. Moon, I trust you completely and I trust myself in return.
4. As you speak, visualize yourself being completely content with yourself, your relationships and your life.
5. Extinguish the candle and trust in yourself and the light of the moon.

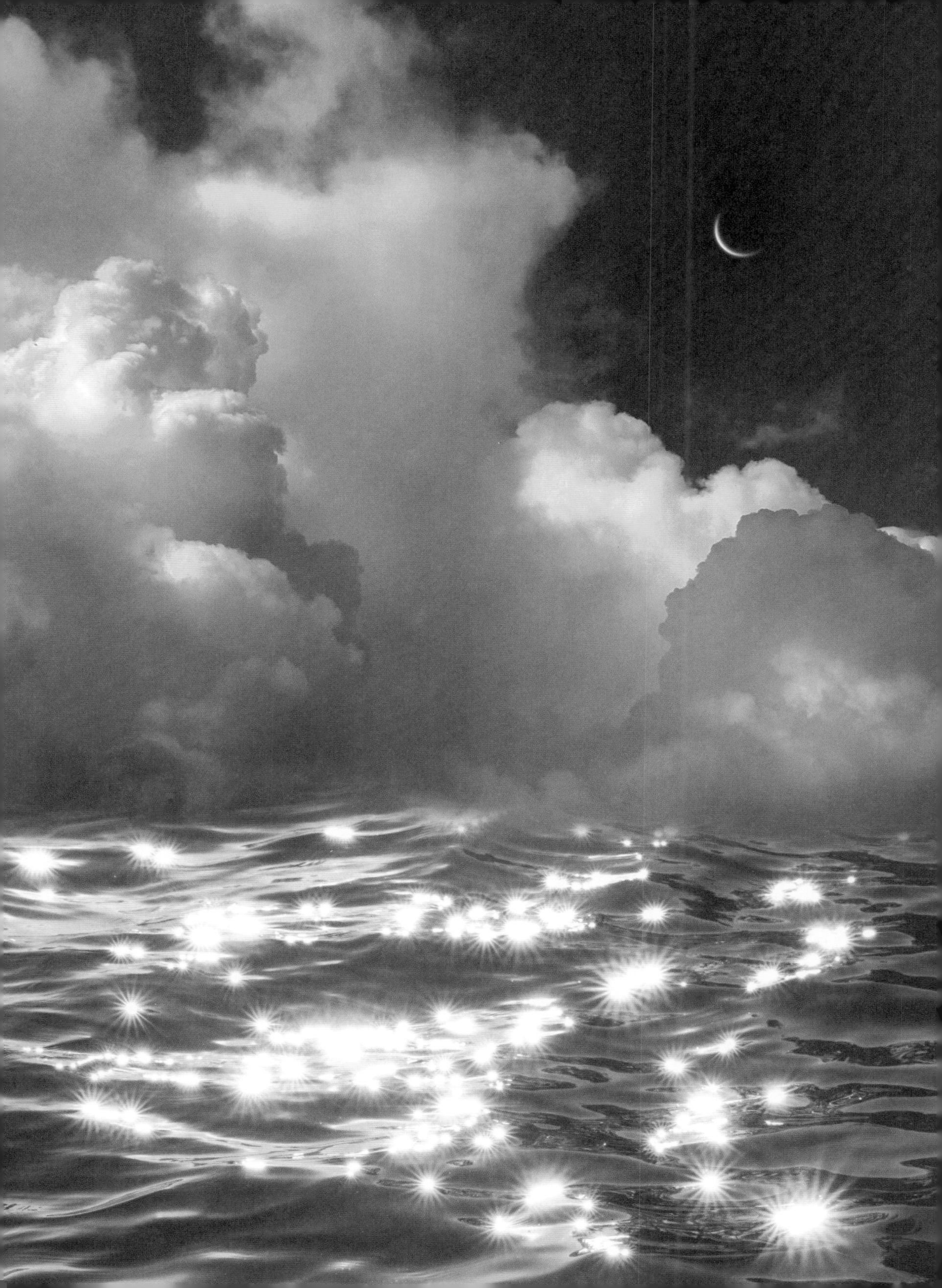

FOR BEST RESULTS
The ideal day to perform this ritual is Friday.

Find New Love

Whether you use this moon fix to help you attract a lover, to strengthen family bonds or simply to bring harmony to other significant friendships and relationships in your life, it can help open your heart to new love and a better understanding of what true love is. Perform this moon fix whenever the moon is new, waxing or full and also in one of the water signs – Cancer, Scorpio and Pisces – to acknowledge the moon's affinity with water and emotions.

YOU WILL NEED
- Rose quartz crystal (ideally heart shaped)
- Moon altar
- Natural moonlight

METHOD
1 Charge your crystal (see page 45). Remember, love can't be seen but it is a powerful force. In the same way, invisible lunar energy is ideally suited to charging crystals.
2 Collect your stone the next morning. Notice how shiny and brand new it looks – that's the moon's power at work for you.
3 Carry your rose quartz with you, or place it on your moon altar, so that every time you see it or touch it, you are reminded to focus on the qualities that define it. Remember that love, compassion, compromise, trust, positivity, humour, respect, friendship, understanding and presence are the defining qualities of happy relationships.
4 Let your rose quartz crystal, freshly charged by the light of the moon, be your daily reminder to see love and moonlight all around you. Let it remind you, too, that love is an active word. You need to show your significant others that you care about them with your actions as well as your words.

MOON CIRCLES These are
places where lunar power can
be captured and turned into a
higher frequency.

Open Communication

This moon fix involves the creation of a moon circle and is designed to increase your eloquence. The secret of a happy relationship is the ability to express how we feel, honestly and tactfully. Sometimes the best form of eloquence can also be silence because it signals that we are giving our full attention to what someone is saying. This moon fix needs to be performed during the waxing phase of the moon, as she increases to her fullness. The ideal days to perform this ritual are Wednesdays or Sundays, when the moon is in one of the air signs – Gemini, Libra or Aquarius – as air is associated with communication.

YOU WILL NEED
- Moonstone crystal
- Other crystals, of your choosing (see page 44)
- Shells, for their association with the tides

METHOD
1 This fix is best performed under the light of the moon in the evening.
2 Place your moonstone crystal in the centre of an imaginary circle and then put other crystals of your choosing or shells to mark the four points of the compass – north, south, east and west, far enough apart that you can stand or sit in it. Imagine that the crystals are linked and form a circle.
3 When you are ready shake your hands to release any negativity and, starting from the east, walk around your circle a few times to calm your body and mind and help your intention tune in to lunar power.
4 Then, pick up the moonstone and sit inside your circle.
5 Holding the crystal in your hand, ask the moon to help you express your feelings honestly to others.
6 Request the moon to fill you with eloquence, ideas and understanding. Then stand up and thank the energy of your moon circle for guidance.

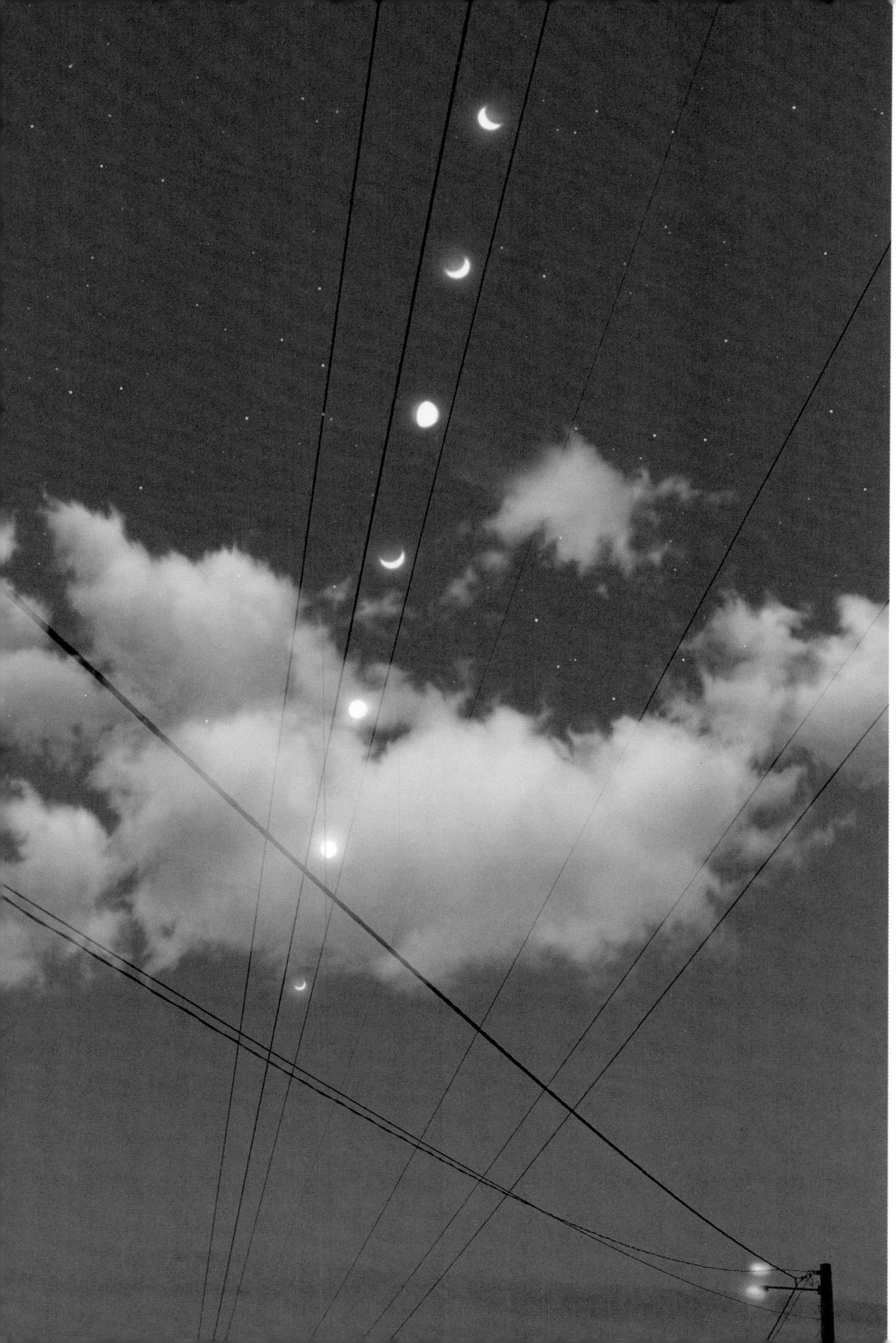

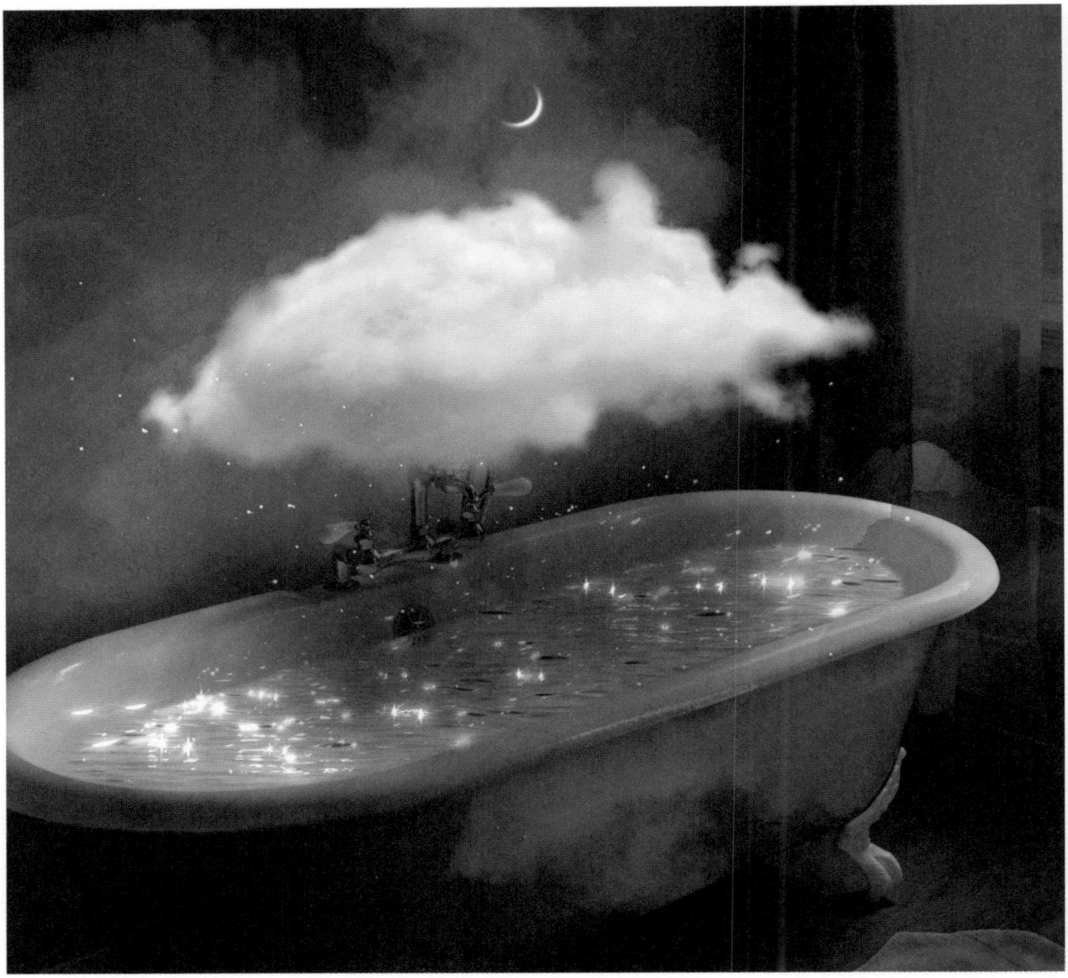

Explore Your Sensuality

This sensual moon fix is designed to add some magical sparkle to your love life. Sensuality is a word frequently associated with sex, but it is more than that. Being sensual is about feeling desirable and enjoying the feel of your body without judgement. The moon is deeply sensual because she is mysterious and has hidden depths. She offers us glimpses of her lunar magic but even when shining in her apparent fullness, she is deeply arcane.

FOR BEST RESULTS
It is most effective when the moon is passing through the fire signs - Aries, Leo and Sagittarius - as fire is associated with passion. Friday also favours this fix.

YOU WILL NEED

- Bubble bath or shower gel
- Bath or shower
- 10 minutes free time (minimum)
- Rose quartz or carnelian crystal
- Jasmine incense
- Matches/lighter
- Relaxing music (optional)
- Body lotion
- Clean, soft/silky nightwear

METHOD

1. When the moon is waxing or full, take a warm and luxurious bubble bath or shower before you go to bed.
2. Place your chosen rose quartz or carnelian crystal nearby, burn the incense and play gentle music, if you wish.
3. Then, for the duration of your bath or shower, become mindfully aware of what your five bodily senses - touch, taste, sight, hearing and smell - are feeling and telling you.
4. Luxuriate in the magical sensual experience of being you for at least 10 minutes and, when you have finished, imagine all limiting anxieties about your body swirling down the drain with the water.
5. Anoint yourself with creamy body lotion and put on night clothes that are soft and silky to the touch.
6. After you have performed this ritual, bear the definition of sensuality as mysterious in mind as you go about your daily life. Remember, the more you focus on the sensuality of enjoying your own body, the more likely it is that it will ignite curiosity and desire in others.

FOR BEST RESULTS The ideal day to perform this ritual is Saturday, especially when the moon is passing through the grounding, healing energies of the earth signs - Taurus, Virgo, Capricorn.

Heal a Broken Heart

If you are suffering from a relationship break-up or grieving for the loss of a loved one, this moon fix can bring comfort and healing to a broken heart. It, therefore, needs to be performed during the waning phase of the moon when the moon journeys from full to dark, because it is about letting go and regaining the strength to move on with your life.

YOU WILL NEED

- Moonstone crystals
- Other crystals of choice, such as clear quartz or jet
- Lavender incense
- Matches/lighter

METHOD

1. The best place to do this ritual is within your moon circle (see method, page 78), when the moon is waning.
2. Place your crystals nearby.
3. Begin by sitting in your circle. Burning lavender incense sticks can encourage a peaceful frame of mind.
4. Repeat the word 'moon' clearly and with conviction until you feel you are in a relaxed enough state to stop chanting and visualize the person you have lost. Wish that person well and thank them for being in your life and teaching you something about yourself. Even if the relationship was toxic or they rejected you, they taught you to value yourself and step away from people who do not value you.
5. Then, feel the love that you gave away to them returning to your heart, bringing you healing, wholeness and strength.
6. End by saying goodbye. Stand up and leave the circle feeling renewed.

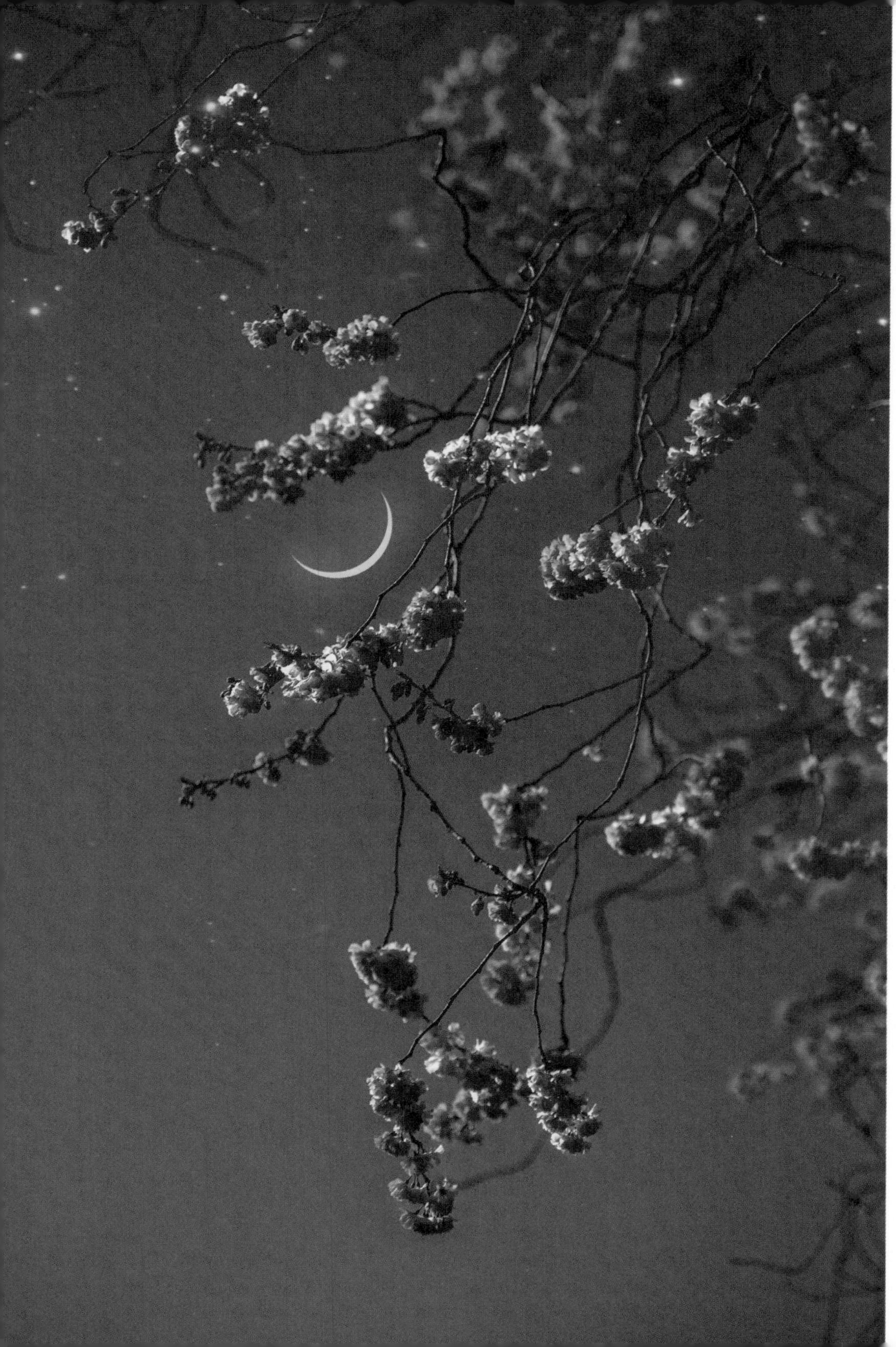

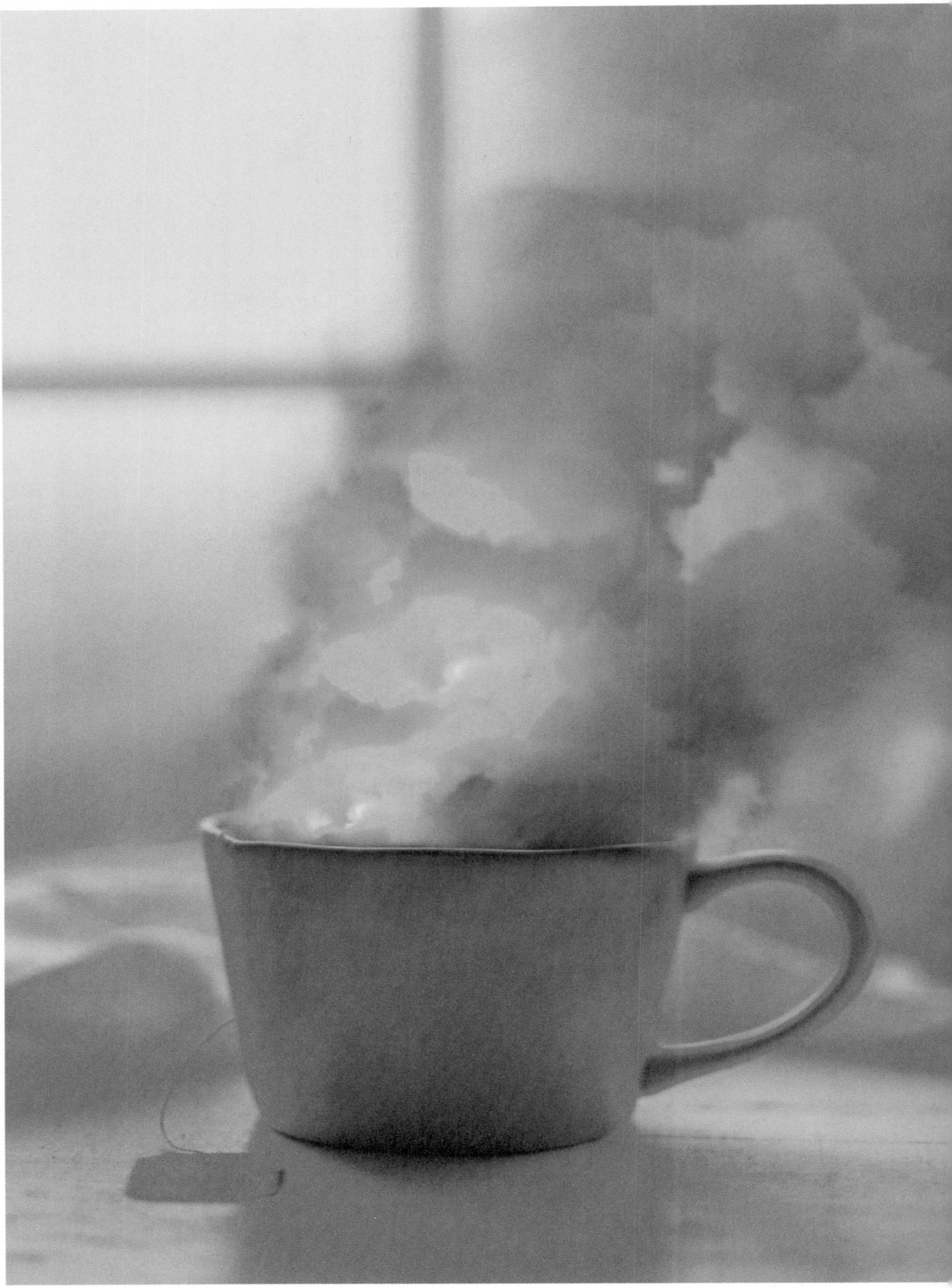

FOR BEST RESULTS This fix is particularly beneficial when performed on a Sunday, Monday, Tuesday or Friday, when the moon is waxing or full.

Practise Self-Gratitude

This fix focuses on the importance of self-love as the foundation stone for positive relationships. One of the best ways to fall in love with yourself and your life is to spend a few moments each day focusing not on what you don't like about yourself and want to improve, but rather on what you already have to be grateful for about yourself.

Lunar Tea Recipe

INGREDIENTS
- 300 ml/10 fl oz/⅔ US pint boiling water
- 1 tbsp chamomile (or hibiscus, lemon balm, rose or lavender) herbal tea
- Infuser
- Teapot
- Mug or cup

METHOD
1. Boil the water.
2. Put your chosen tea/flowers into an infuser, place in the teapot and pour boiling water over it.
3. Leave to brew for five minutes, then pour into a mug or cup.
4. When your drink is ready, sit beside a window and look out at the moon. If you can't see her, imagine her there in the night sky shining for you.
5. Then, as you drink your tea, say out loud three things about yourself that you feel grateful for. It might simply be the fact that you like the way your hair looked today or that you held a door open for someone.
6. Every day that you do this under the light of the moon, notice how flexing your gratitude muscle changes the way you think and feel about yourself – for the better.

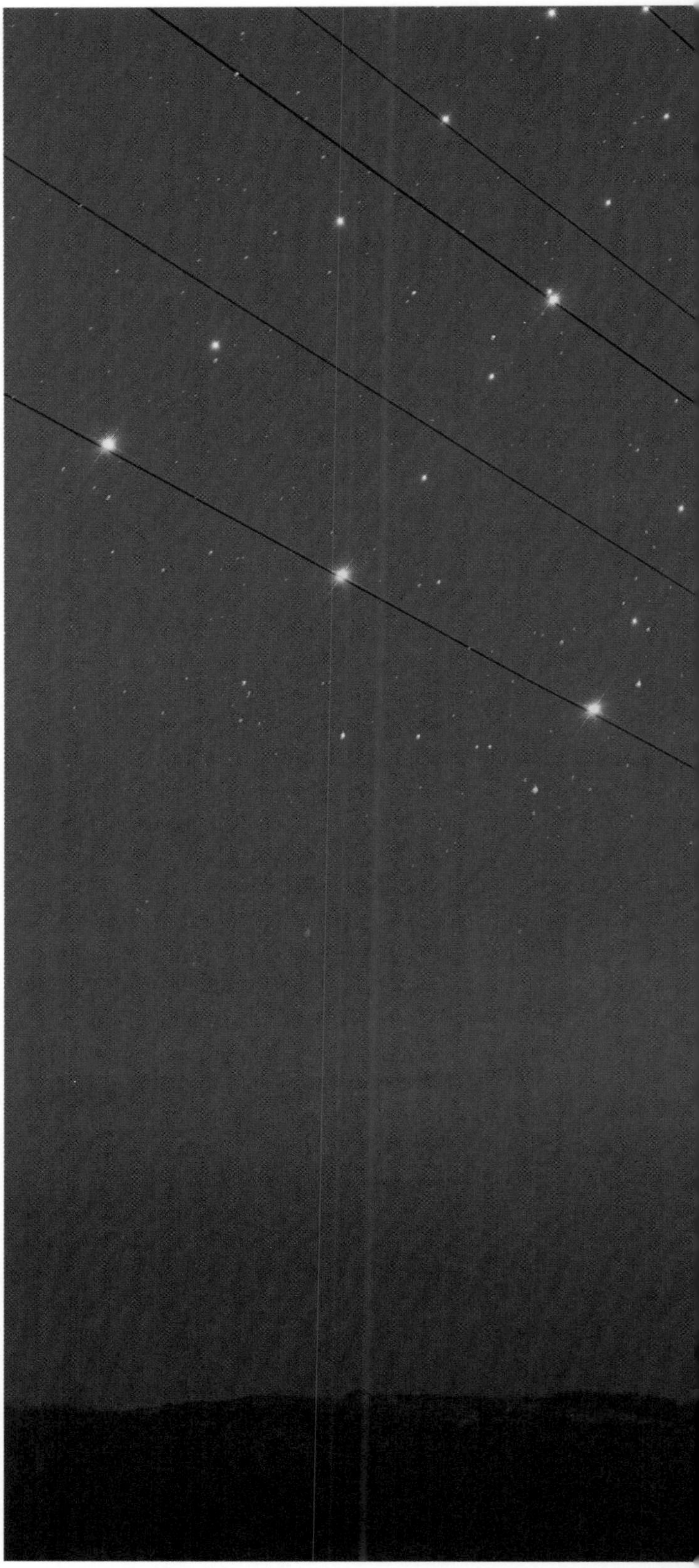

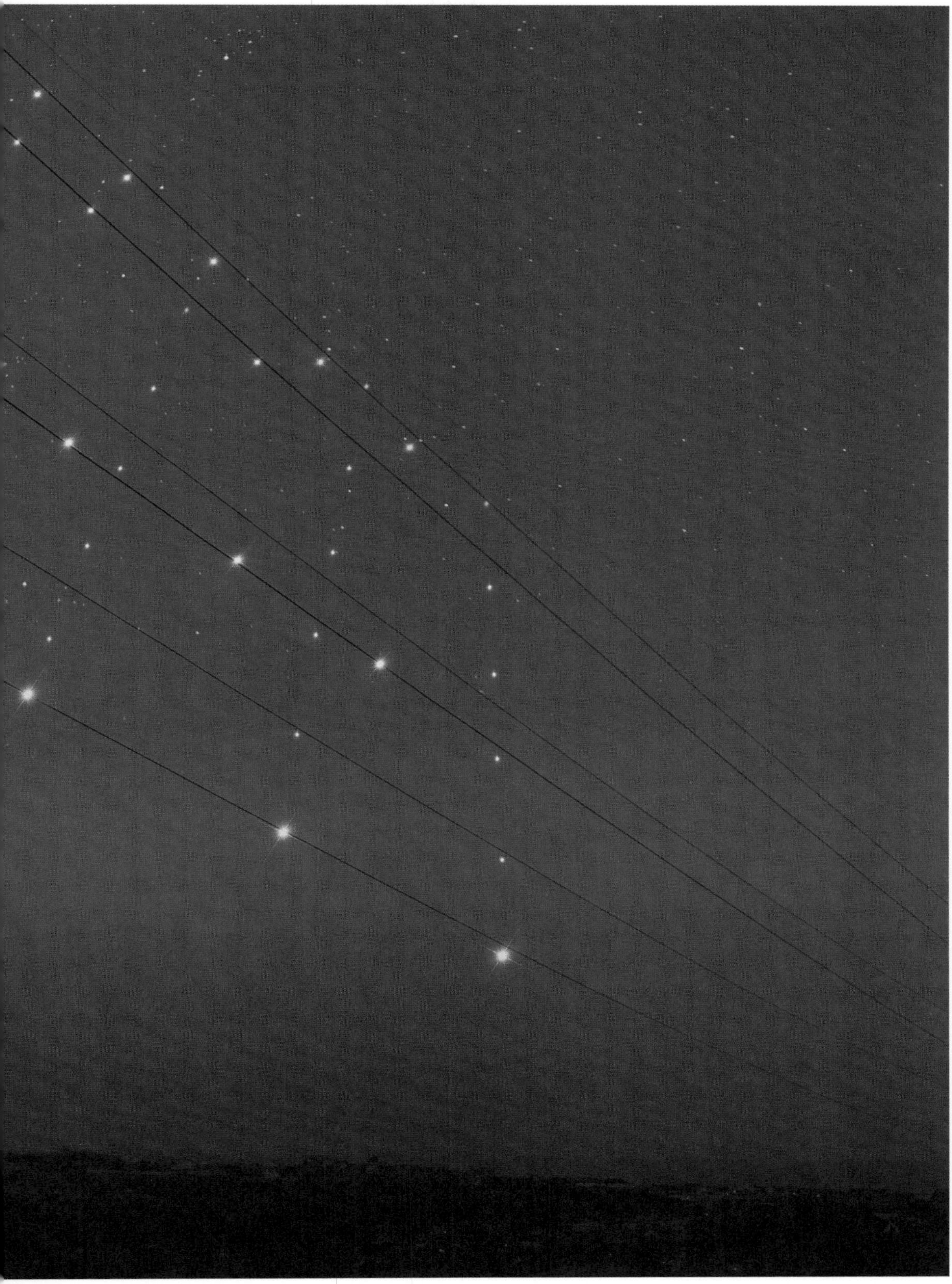

HEALTH AND WELLNESS

Whenever the moon moves from one phase to another, this affects not just your thoughts and feelings but also your body. The moon fixes in this section are all designed to align your physical energies with the moon's influences throughout each lunar cycle, to improve your health – from finding help with kicking your unhealthy habits, to dealing with anxiety and even boosting your body confidence. They should be used in addition to – and not as a substitute for – any current medical treatment you may be on or advice from your doctor.

FOR BEST RESULTS
Connect with the increasing energies of the waxing and full moon phases to increase your own health.

Good Health Ritual

Our bodies are almost three-quarters water. Water is life. Yet most of us fail to pay enough attention to the quality and quantity of the water we drink. This fix will not just help you absorb lunar energy but also remind you how crucial water is for your health and well-being. This particular ritual can be done on any day of the week.

YOU WILL NEED

- Empty drinking bottles, preferably glass
- Fresh water (enough for your typical daily water intake)

METHOD

1. In the periods when the moon is waxing and full, every night, before you go to bed, fill your bottles with clean, fresh water.
2. Then, leave the bottles overnight on your window ledge indoors, under the light of the moon.
3. The following day, when you get up, create a ritual of drinking a glass of moon-infused water first thing in the morning immediately. Notice how energizing and luxurious it feels to drink moon water and absorb lunar power into every part of your being.
4. Then, throughout the day continue to drink your sacred moon water until the bottle is empty.
5. Let this moon fix encourage you to keep drinking enough water when the moon is waning. Then, when it is waxing again and increasing, you can seize the opportunity to replenish your moon water supply and further boost your health.

ENHANCE YOUR MOON WORK

You can make this moon fix more potent by placing a rose quartz crystal nearby, as well as by burning lemon balm or citrus incense.

Boost Body Confidence

If you don't feel comfortable with your body, working with the moon is essential therapy. Lunar energy exerts a positive influence on your health. You can therefore work with the moon to feel better about your body and the way you look and feel. This fix should be performed when the moon is new and waxing and can be done on any day of the week, but Tuesday, Saturday and Sunday are recommended.

YOU WILL NEED

- Picture of the moon
- Mirror

METHOD

1. Every evening when the moon is new and waxing be sure to take a few moments to gaze up at her. If you can't see the moon, gaze at some pictures from this book.
2. Then, with your thoughts filled with those images of the natural beauty of the moon, take a look in a mirror and stare deeply into your own eyes with the same sense of reverence. As you look at your own eyes, notice how beautiful they are. Notice every unique detail.
3. Then say out loud the following affirmation and mean what you say, 'On this night, with the beauty of the moon above me, I (your name here) love my beautiful body and I promise to take the very best care of it.'
4. You will probably feel odd talking to yourself in this way, especially if you often tell yourself negative things. If you don't believe what you are saying, that's fine – just pretend that you do. Notice how talking out loud to your body in this loving way raises your motivation and energy levels.

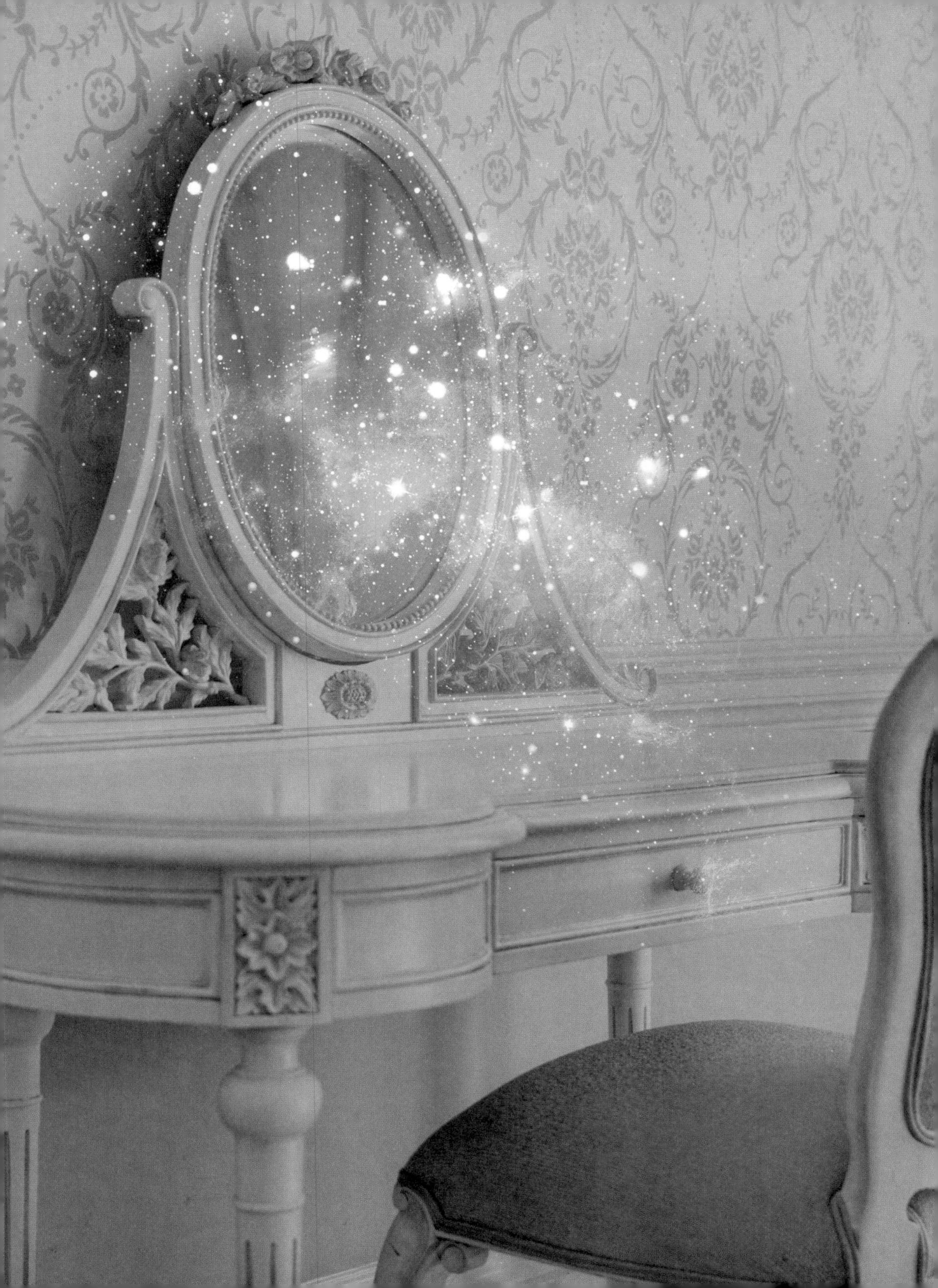

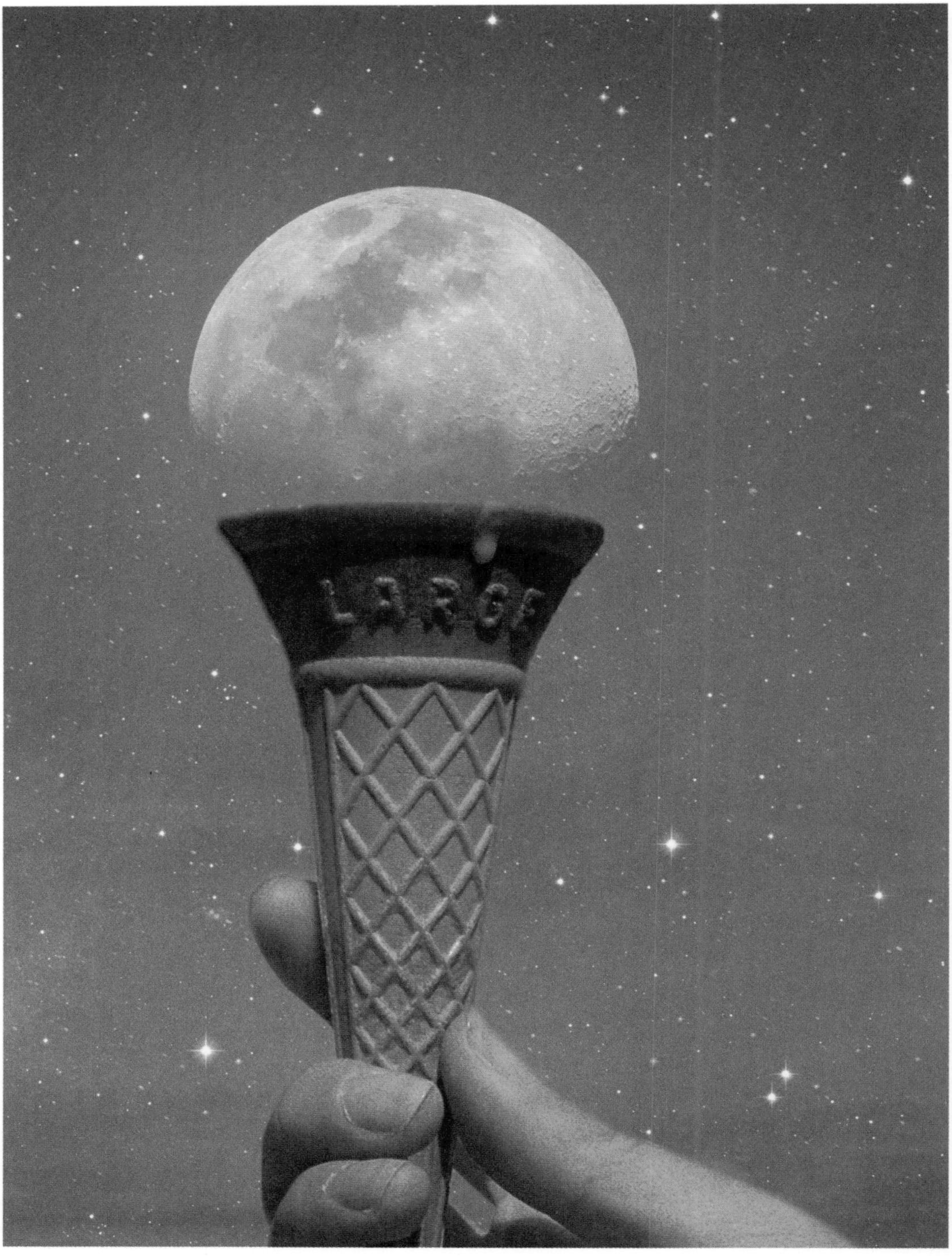
LARGE

FOR BEST RESULTS Sunday is the ideal day for this moon fix, and whenever the moon passes through health-orientated sign Virgo is particularly beneficial.

Overcome Compulsion

Excessive behaviour of any sort can destroy your health and well-being. Whether you are addicted to fast food, chocolate, alcohol, smoking or to watching too much TV, this moon fix will help give you strength to cut down on unhealthy habits. Aligning yourself with the energies of the moon encourages you to listen more to what your body is telling you when it craves something. It needs to be performed when the moon is waning, as you are aiming to decrease compulsive behaviour while the moon is also decreasing.

YOU WILL NEED

- Amethyst crystal
- Pen
- Blank piece of paper
- A tool for digging, such as as a small trowel or a spoon

METHOD

1. Place an amethyst crystal nearby.
2. Write down on a piece of paper the excessive or unhealthy behaviour you want to release.
3. Be factual. Don't judge or bring yourself down. Acknowledge that your compulsive behaviour has been your coping mechanism, but now that you are working with the moon, you no longer need it. You can let it go.
4. When you have finished, go outside and try to see the moon. If you can't see her, know that she is there.
5. Then tear up the piece of paper into as many tiny pieces as possible and, as you do so, ask the moon to strengthen your resolve.
6. Bury the pieces of paper in the ground in three different places. As you dispose of it, trust that the moon will replace the void with inner strength and a glowing feeling of wholeness and well-being.

ENHANCE YOUR MOON WORK Place an amethyst beside your bedside as you sleep and dream to enhance this moon fix.

Find Insight in Dreams

Sometimes our thoughts can make us feel unhealthy or cause mental fogginess. This moon fix is for clarity of mind. It needs to be performed during a full moon, which offers an incredible opportunity for clarity, insight and focus. It is a powerful time to see things clearly and bring your awareness to your dreams and the wonderful insights about you they can offer.

YOU WILL NEED

- Blank notebook
- Pen
- Torch

METHOD

1 Before you go to bed be sure to place a notebook, pen and torch beside your bed.
2 Take a look outside at the full moon if you can and ask her to send you clarity about your life in a night vision.
3 Before you drift off to sleep, tell yourself you are going to dream and you will be able to recall your dream. Say this out loud if you can.
4 When you wake up the next morning, or if you wake in the night, write down any images or feelings that you can recall as soon as possible. Write in the present tense and don't try to make sense of them as you write.
5 Later in the day, re-read what you have written and try to see if you can make any associations.
6 If you can't recall anything when you wake up, simply write that down and perhaps some images will jump into your mind later. The more you think about or mention your dreams, even when you can't remember them, the more likely you are to recall them in coming days. Just like working with the moon, your dreaming mind thrives and grows stronger the more attention you pay to it.

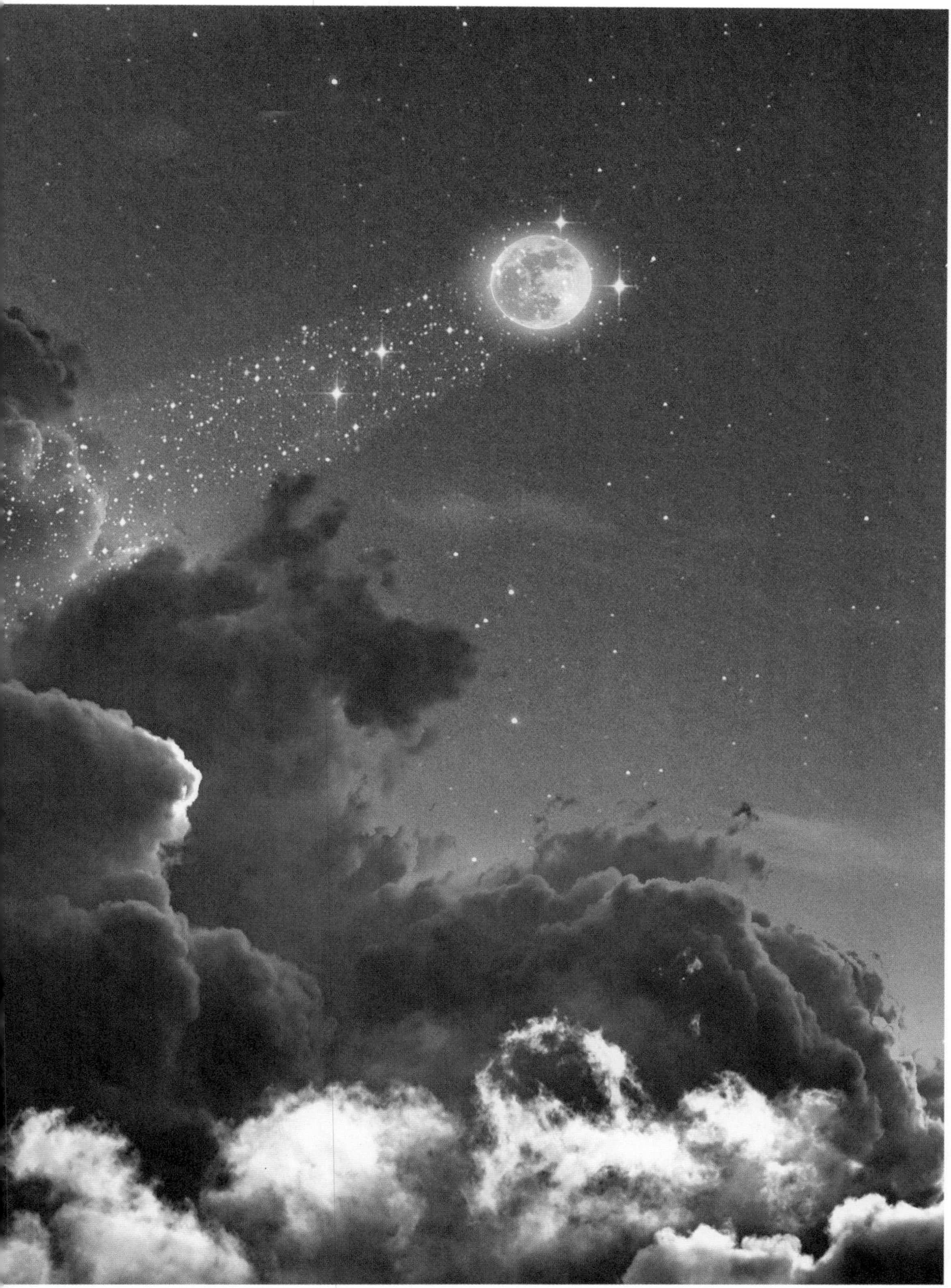

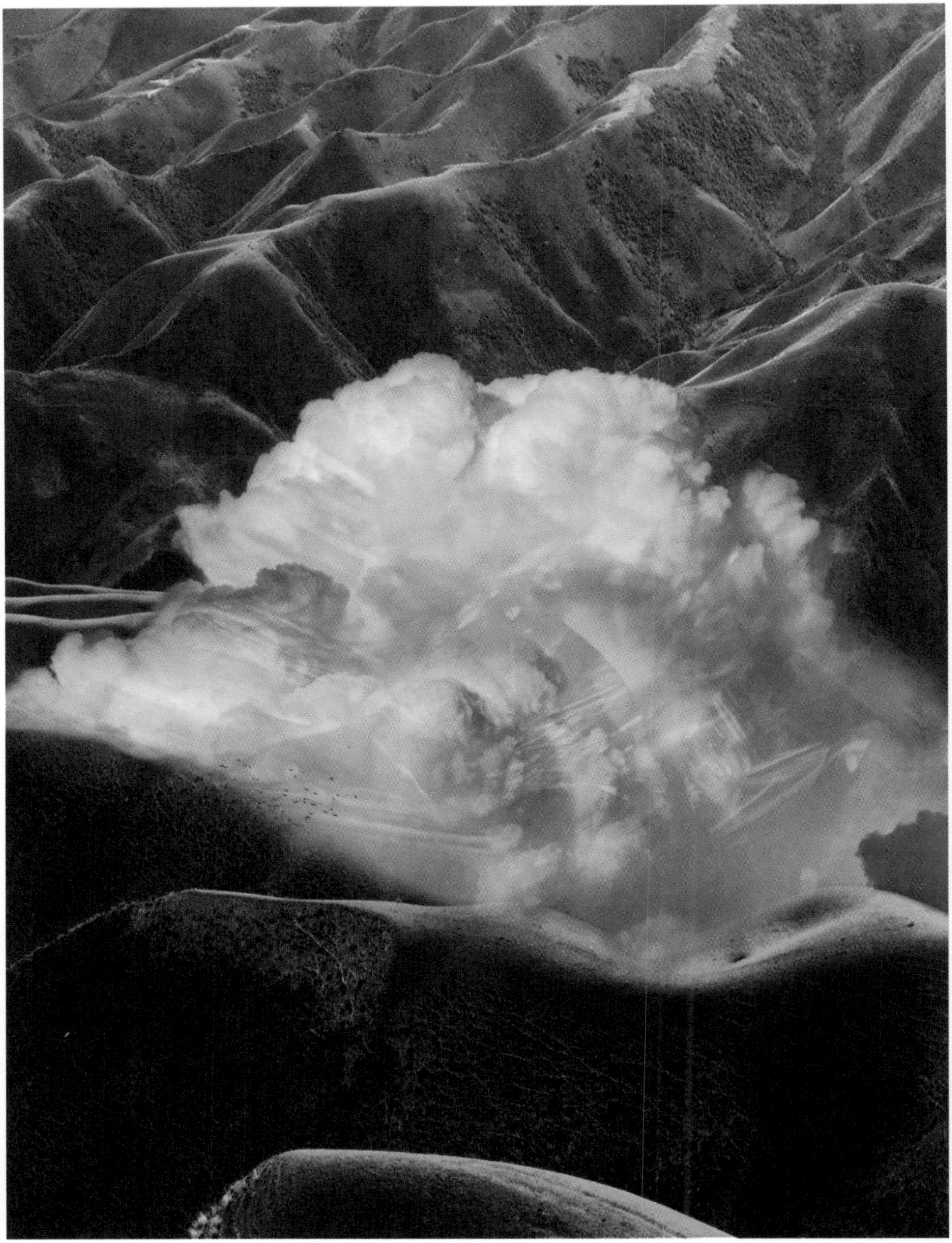

ENHANCE YOUR MOON WORK Green crystals are perfect for stress reduction as their beautiful green colour is nourishing, healing and nurturing. Try aventurine, aquamarine or malachite with this fix.

Anxiety Antidote

Stress can cause headaches, poor digestion, depression and insomnia and can also significantly increase the risk of disease. Stress reduction is a vital part of any health-boosting programme. You need to perform this moon fix during the waning phase of the moon because it is about decreasing your stress levels as the moon itself decreases. This moon phase, particularly when it passes through the health-conscious sign of Virgo and the transformative sign of Scorpio, is an ideal time. This fix is designed to help promote calm, but if anxiety is impacting your everyday life, there are a range of services and health professionals who can offer help.

YOU WILL NEED

- Aventurine, or another crystal that is green in colour
- Green items of clothing

METHOD

1   During this moon phase, try to wear your green crystal or carry it around with you to reduce feelings of stress and to give you the resilience and inner strength to cope with it.

2   Wearing green items of clothing during this period can also help. Like crystals, colours have energetic vibrations that can help focus and direct energy. Green is universally believed to have healing powers, physically, mentally and emotionally. So, to ease stress and draw down the well-being of the moon during her waning phase, simply go green.

FOR BEST RESULTS It should be performed by women when the moon is new and when it is full, and by men when the moon passes through the signs of Aries and Libra.

Balance Your Hormones

Your body is intimately connected to the rhythms of nature and the moon. Aligning yourself with the natural ebb and flow of the moon's phases is a gentle but powerful way to balance your hormones and your natural cycles. It is ideal for women whose cycles are irregular, but it can benefit anyone: balanced hormones are essential for everyone's good health.

YOU WILL NEED

- Some natural land and sky
- Bare feet

METHOD

1. Each month, at the appropriate time (see box above) walk barefoot outside for a few minutes during the day. Make sure you are somewhere safe, and have checked the ground for anything dangerous. Walking barefoot is a healing technique called 'earthing' because by doing this you are absorbing the earth's healing energy through the soles of your feet.
2. As you walk, mindfully reflect only on your connection to nature through the soles of your feet, and your connection to the energy of the moon through your emotions and the water that makes up a large part of your body. Should distracting thoughts come into your mind, observe them and don't judge. Let them pass through you.
3. If you prefer not to walk barefoot, simply head outside and do some cloud watching, as it will have similar connecting-to-nature and balancing and healing effects.
4. Spend a few moments reflecting on how walking barefoot or gazing at the clouds connects you to nature both on earth and in space. Feel yourself in flow with nature and the moon and stars, and honour the natural connection of your life and your body with the moon.

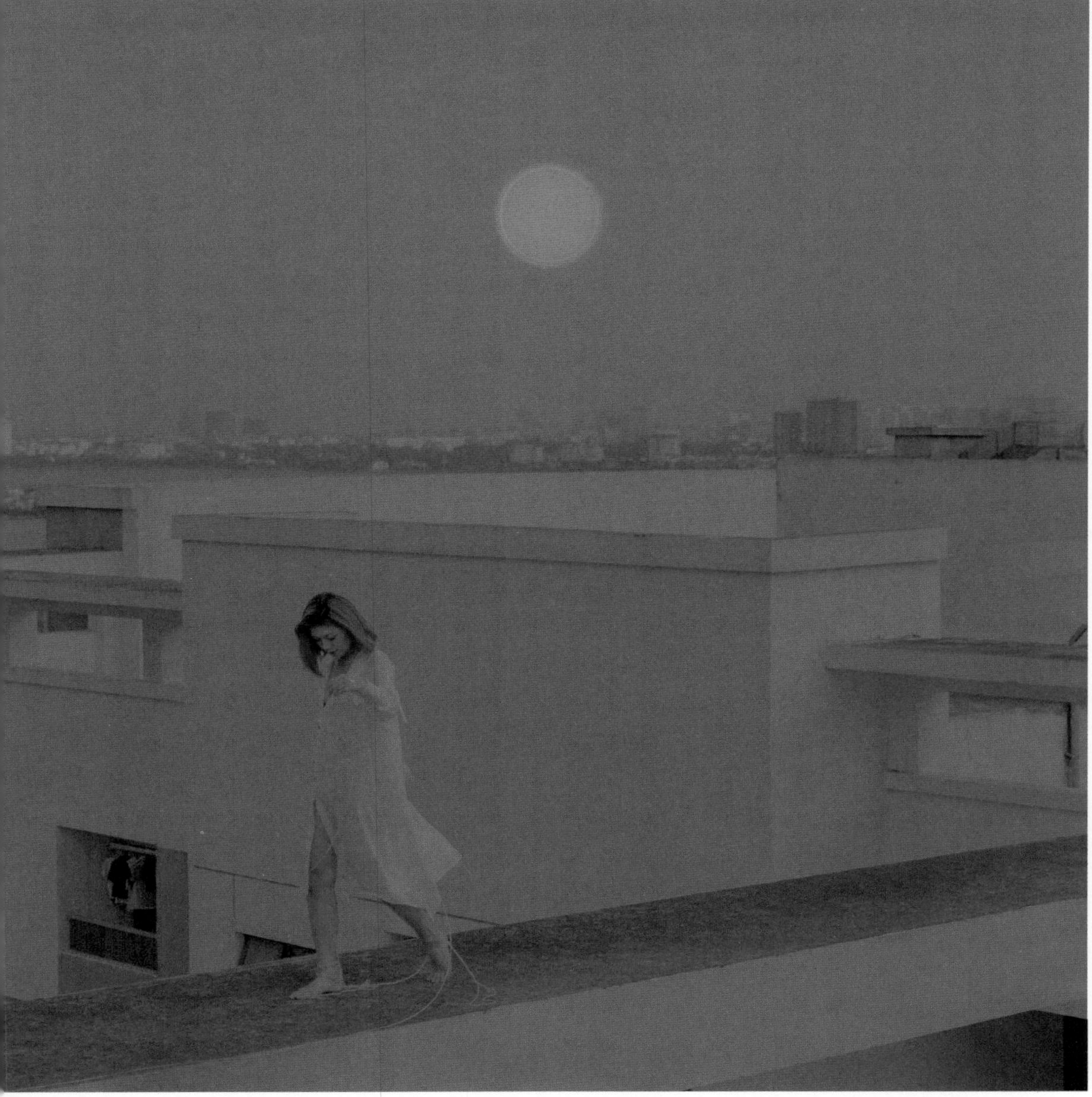

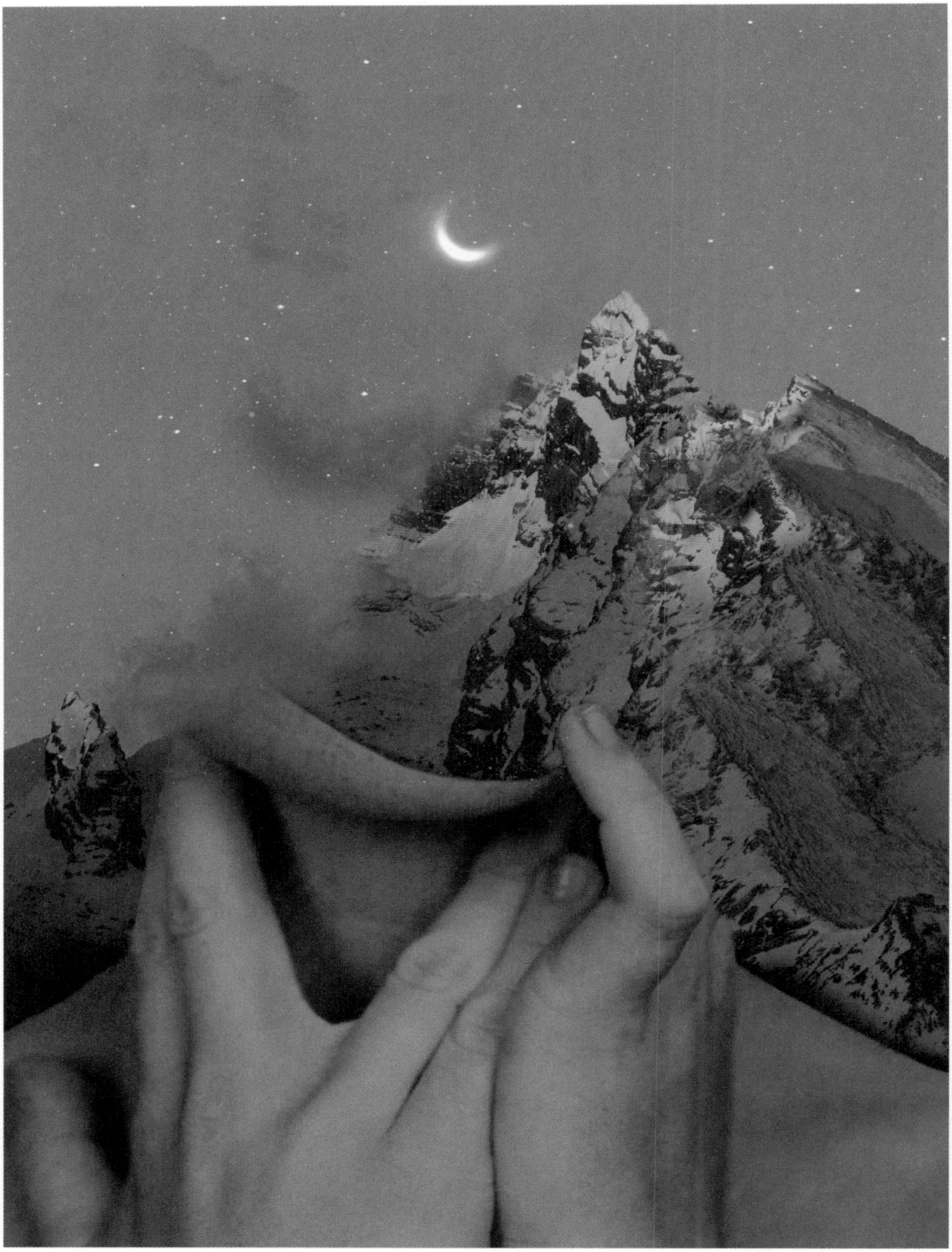

ENHANCE YOUR MOON WORK Placing a fuchsite or clear quartz crystal nearby, or carrying those crystals with you, can help add a greater energetic dimension to this fix.

Strengthen Your Constitution

Most of us only really appreciate our health when we feel weakened by disease or injury. This moon fix will ensure you don't take your health for granted and help boost your immunity. It encourages vibrations of physical strength and wellness. It can be performed on any day of the lunar cycle but is particularly beneficial during the waxing phase when the moon increases in the same way that you would like to increase your good health.

YOU WILL NEED
- Drinking glass
- Moon water (see method, page 89)
- A quiet place

METHOD
1 Take a glass of moon water and sit somewhere quietly with the glass in front of you.
2 Look at the water and visualize the healing energy of moonlight captured in it.
3 Then focus on what your body needs right now. Ask yourself what self-care routines are helping to nourish and heal your body. If you aren't taking the best care of your body, ask yourself what is stopping you from doing so.
4 Now dip two of your fingers into the moon water. Touch your heart and say, 'My heart is strong.' Next, touch your forehead and say, 'My mind is strong.'
5 Then dip your fingers in the water again, stand up and touch the top of your head and say, 'My body is strong.' Visualize the light of the moon surging down through your body, giving it strength.
6 Then thank the moon for your health, go outside and pour your moon water onto the earth.

Boost Health with Lunar-Friendly Foods

Choosing foods that are lunar friendly (see recipe opposite) will nurture your connection to the moon and, at the same time, boost your health. You are what you eat. The nutrients in food nourish and heal you, and can help ward off disease. It doesn't matter what day of the week or which phase the moon is in to get the benefits of this fix.

To get the most out of this fix, focus not just on what you eat, but also the way you eat. Eating quickly in a stressful environment can cause digestive upsets and nutritional deficiencies that can lead to poor health. When it comes to the main meal of your day, be sure to place your moonstone crystal on the table beside you as you eat. This will bring a sense of peace and healing to your meal. Then, put on some slow, calming music. Listen to it and time your bites to what you are hearing. You will notice it really slows you down.

LUNAR-FRIENDLY FOOD How can you tell when a food is lunar-friendly? It will be natural, wholesome and good for you. If it's more indulgent, working with the moon will help you learn to savour it in moderation.

New Moon Salad

SERVES 4

The new moon is the time to keep your meals light, wholesome and fresh. Salads and vegetable-based dishes are ideal, so why not try this delicious New Moon Salad? (For a waning moon recipe, see page 150; for a waxing and full moon recipe, see page 151; and for another full moon recipe, see page 67.)

INGREDIENTS

- 4 cooked chicken breasts
- Alternatives to chicken: 500 g/1 lb 2 oz/4 cups mushrooms, grilled, seasoned and brushed with olive oil; 2 x 200 g/5 oz cans tuna, drained
- 1 medium crisp lettuce
- 1 small bunch spring onions/scallions
- 3–4 tbsp mayonnaise
- 4 tbsp soy sauce
- 2 tbsp sesame seeds
- 3 tbsp grated almonds
- good squeeze of lemon
- salt/pepper, to taste
- bread sticks, to serve

METHOD

1. Shred the chicken or alternative ingredient and set aside.
2. Next, shred the lettuce and slice the spring onions/scallions into thin pieces. Put them to one side.
3. Then, in a bowl, combine the mayonnaise and soy sauce with 2 tablespoons of water. Mix well.
4. Add the chicken, lettuce and spring onions, followed by the rest of the ingredients, and toss the salad well.
5. Serve with the bread sticks.

ENERGY AND INSPIRATION

Feeling burnt-out is a familiar complaint in today's fast-paced world. There are constant demands on our energy levels and vitality drainers surround us. However, aligning your personal energy with lunar inspiration can help.

Every month, the moon's energy ebbs and flows according to a consistent and steady pattern that does not deviate. You can count on the moon. By contrast, human energy is inconsistent and your emotions are also constantly shifting. Tuning in to the moon's predicable energy shifts can make everything in your life flow more effortlessly. Use the moon fixes in this section to naturally boost your personal energy levels and put a spring in your step and a twinkle in your eye.

FOR BEST RESULTS
Choose an essential oil that complements the current moon phase (see page 47).

Energy Boost

Energy is the invisible force that animates everything and everyone. Energy is life. Sadly, many of us settle for energy levels that are lacklustre, but low energy levels are not normal. Working with the energy of the moon can replenish depleted energy levels so you start your day feeling glad to be alive. It is a simple daily reminder to be grateful for the vital energy that is your life. This energy boosting moon fix is one that can be repeated every day in the lunar cycle.

YOU WILL NEED
- Bath or shower
- Essential oil

METHOD
1 Transform your morning showering or washing routine into a daily moon ritual. As you wash, simply visualize the light of the moon shining onto you and then see it floating all around you.
2 When you have finished washing yourself or when you see water draining away, imagine all energy-depleting stress draining away.
3 When you have dried yourself, anoint your wrists with a tiny drop of moon phase-friendly essential oil.
4 You are now fully charged with lunar energy and ready to start your day.
5 If your energy levels dip during the day you can perform this lunar visualization whenever you wash your hands.

FOR BEST RESULTS The
energies of specific days may
influence how you perform this
fix (see page 38).

Clear Your Focus

Just as the moon lights up the night sky, meaningful work or having a passion
and purpose in life can light up our lives. If you don't enjoy your work or have
life goals that don't fulfil you, it can be very hard to feel motivated. This fix
will give your energy levels a serious boost by helping you focus clearly on
what really matters to you. It should be performed during the new moon.

YOU WILL NEED

- Citrine crystal
- White candle
- Green candle
- Matches/lighter
- Relaxing music (optional)
- Notebook
- Pen

METHOD

1 Place a citrine crystal nearby as it helps promote clarity.
2 Light one white and one green candle. White is for clarity and green is for
   harmony. You might want to play relaxing music in the background.
3 Shake your hands to release any negative energy.
4 Visualize the new moon at the start of her new cycle, bursting with
   energy and potential. As you visualize the moon's energy flowing through
   you, ask her to help you answer the following three questions:
   - What do I love to do?
   - What am I good at?
   - What does the world need or how can I serve others?
5 You may want to jot down in your notebook whatever illumination comes
   to you. Don't try to force anything. Asking these questions under the light
   of the new moon will encourage your mind to seek out answers in the
   days ahead. Questions are what nurture focus and creativity.
6 Safely extinguish your candles when you have finished and thank the
   moon for her illumination.

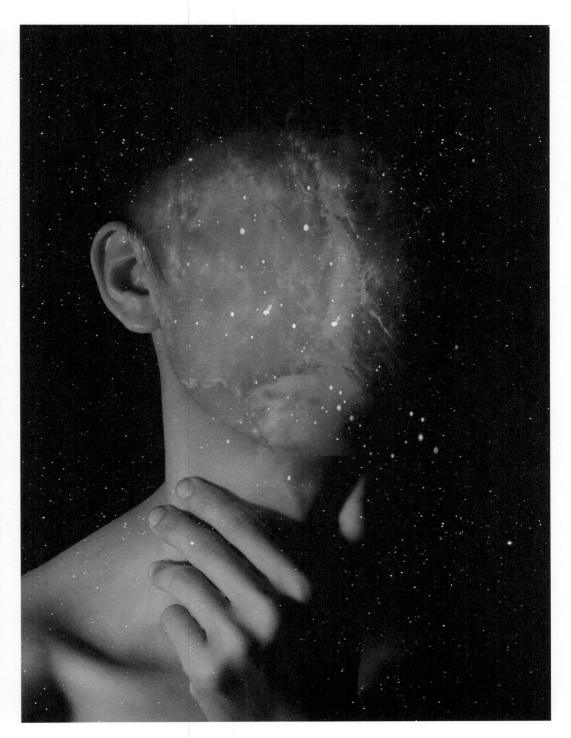

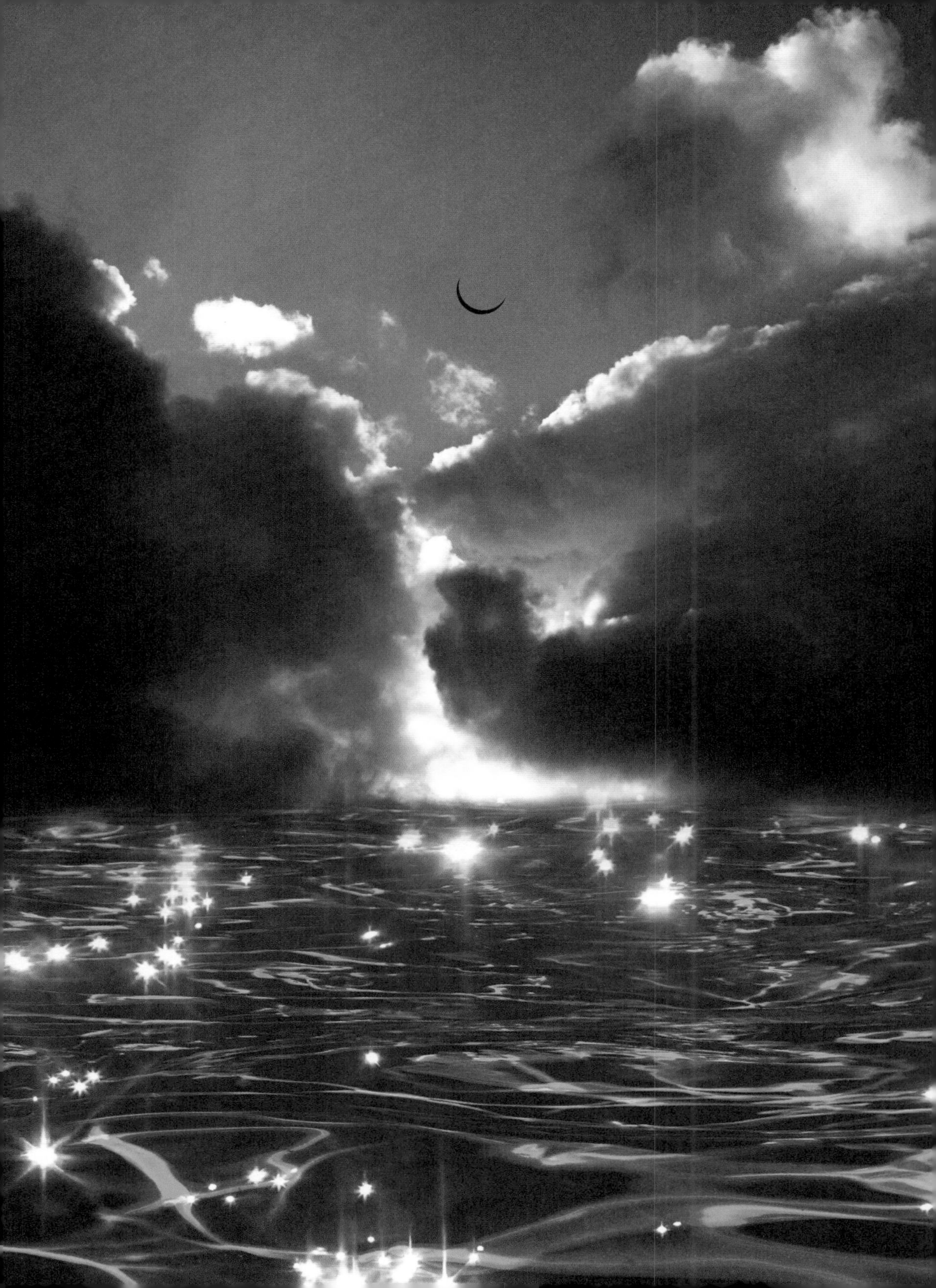

FOR BEST RESULTS Perform this fix during the new or waxing moon phases. They signify new beginnings and a new chapter in your life, helping you connect to your most confident self.

Ignite Self-Confidence

There is nothing more energy sapping than low levels of confidence. Lack of confidence and self-belief holds you back on every level. It stops you stepping outside your comfort zone, which is where all the personal growth and magic begin. Do remember that confidence is not something that happens overnight though. It takes time to grow your self-belief.

YOU WILL NEED

- Blue lace agate crystal
- Prayer

METHOD

1. Place your blue agate crystal in front of you and study its soft blue and white hues. Notice how they are like the beautiful hues of the moon.
2. Pick the crystal up. Spend a few moments thinking about things you have done in the last few days that you are proud of. It doesn't have to be anything major.
3. If you can't think of anything, let this incentivize you to repeat this exercise in a few days.
4. Then say out loud the following prayer: 'Mother moon as your light increases this month, let confidence also grow in me. Give me the power to remember what is strong about me whenever I lack self-belief.'
5. Visualize the light of the moon surrounding you. Feel your confidence growing and lighting up the room you are in.
6. Thank the moon and feel lunar strength growing within you.

TRIED AND TESTED
Farming and gardening according
to the moon and her phases is a
centuries-old practice.

Cultivate Self-Discipline

Successful people are highly disciplined people. All the moon fixes in this
book encourage self-discipline and this fix, in particular, turns the spotlight
brightly on improving this quality by encouraging you to keep your own lunar
herbal garden. The moon's gravitational pull connects to the earth as well as
the oceans. So, even if you don't have a garden and are caring for your herbs
in pots filled with soil and nourished with water, aligning your herbal care
routine with the phases of the moon will still make a difference.

YOU WILL NEED
- Garden or indoor pot plants
- Lunar plants and herbs (see page 47) you can plant and grow

METHOD
1 Plant and fertilize your seeds when it is new moon and waxing.
2 Be sure to tend to your plants and herbs daily, weeding, watering and
   feeding them as required and ensuring they get the right amount of
   daylight. If they don't need much tending to physically, send them your
   loving energy.
3 Prune and harvest the plants when the moon is waning.
4 Seeing your lunar garden flourish is one of the most rewarding ways to
   tap into lunar power every day. If you want something, you have to put in
   the time and effort to make it happen. There are no short cuts. You need
   to find the self-discipline to tend to it regularly.

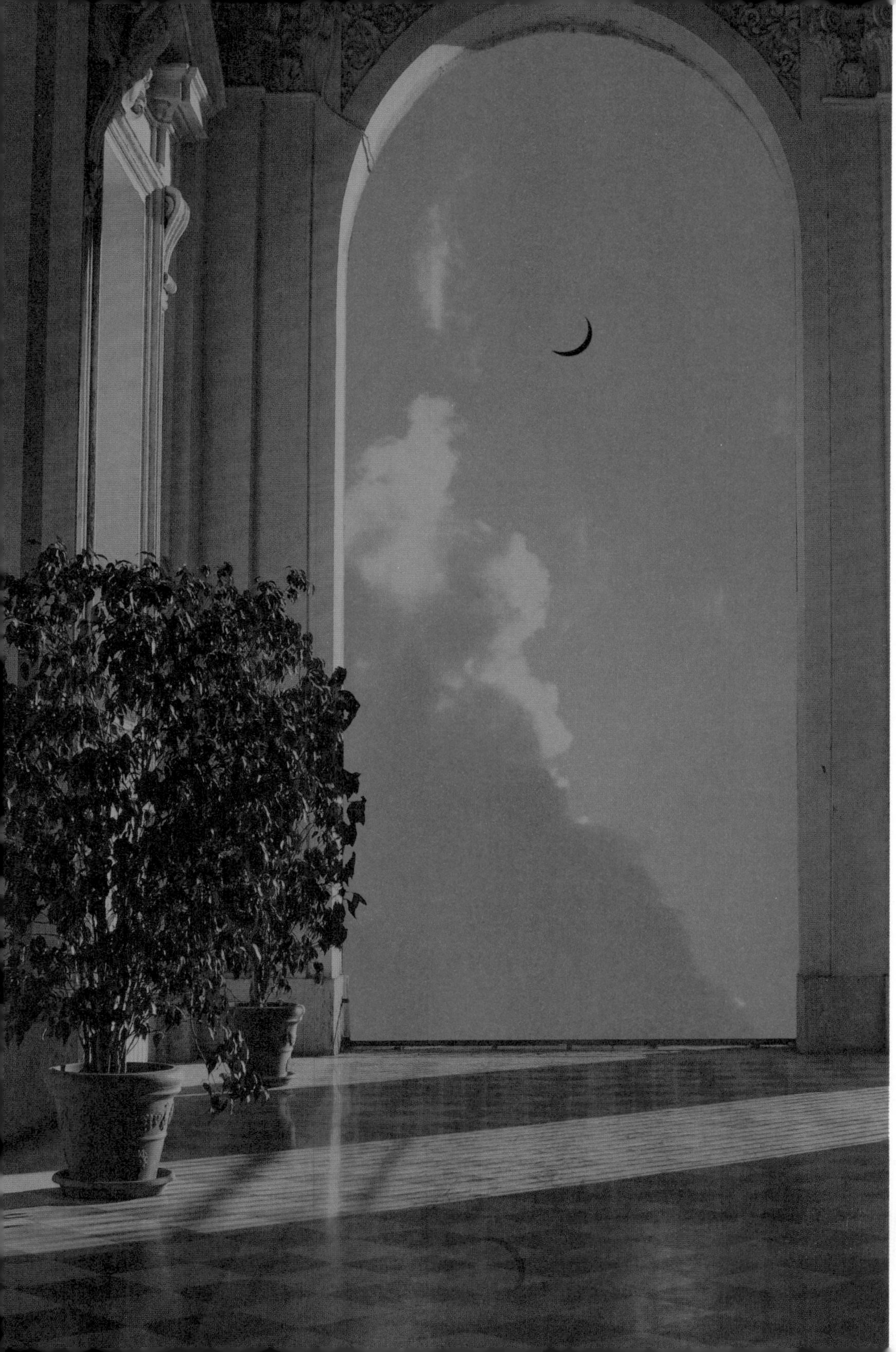

FIRE SIGNS These are Aries, Leo and Sagittarius.

Get Fired Up

Knowing which sign the moon is currently in can help you understand why your energy levels can sometimes shift inexplicably. This moon fix is dedicated to those days of the month when the moon is shifting through the fire signs to help you tune in to the confident and vibrant productive energy associated with this element. Fire was once believed to be a divine gift from the gods to humankind and it is associated with the heat of the sun and, therefore, life. Although fire can bring with it a tendency to be impatient and impulsive, it can also significantly boost confidence and motivation.

YOU WILL NEED
- Quiet, dark place
- White candle
- Candle holder
- Matches/lighter

METHOD
1 When the moon is passing through a fire sign find a dark and quiet space.
2 Place a simple, plain white candle in a candle holder.
3 Sit in complete silence for a few moments and pay attention to your breathing.
4 When you feel calm, light the candle. Do this as smoothly as possible.
5 Now simply watch the flame for about a minute. Don't stare intensely, just gaze quietly. Then blow out the candle.
6 Close your eyes and look at the image of the flame on your retina. Focus all your attention on that.
7 Keep focusing calmly on that vibrant image until it fades.
8 Open your eyes and feel the calm confidence and warm glow of fire ignite within you and let it bring added sparkle, motivation and an adventurous spirit to your daily life.

AIR SIGNS These are Gemini, Libra and Aquarius.

Unleash Creativity

This moon fix is dedicated to those days of the month when the moon is shifting through the air signs to help you tune in to the creative and innovative energy associated with this element. Air is a pure element. It is the invisible source of life that is weightless and fast moving. It pervades our bodies and is our breath, our life. Although air can be fickle and distracting, it is also the source of all sound and communication and can inspire flights of tremendous creativity and eloquence.

YOU WILL NEED

- A clear view of the sky
- An open mind

METHOD

1. Find a window with a clear view of the sky and open the window. Better still, if you have a safe area to do so, go outside, lie down and look up at the sky.
2. Avoid looking directly at the sun.
3. Look at the sky and watch the clouds changing shape for 3–5 minutes.
4. Focus your awareness on the clouds and feel the air on your skin gently touching your face. If there is no breeze, focus mindfully on your breath. Let distracting thoughts float away. Your attention is on watching and feeling air.
5. If you can catch a glimpse of the moon when you are cloud watching, all the better.
6. Finish your cloud watching by taking a deep breath in and an even deeper breath out and as you do, feel the eloquence, creativity and innovative spirit of air take flight within you.

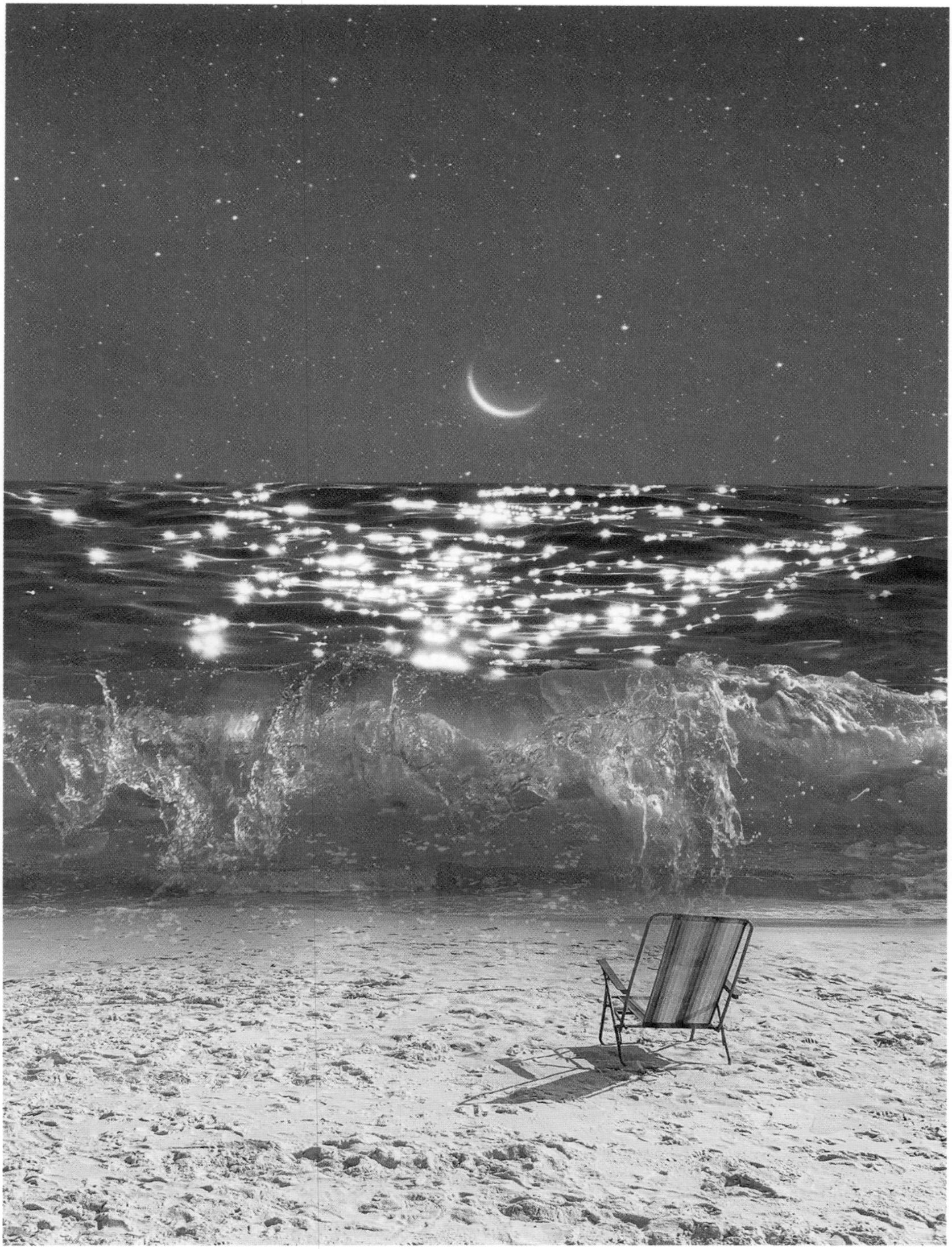

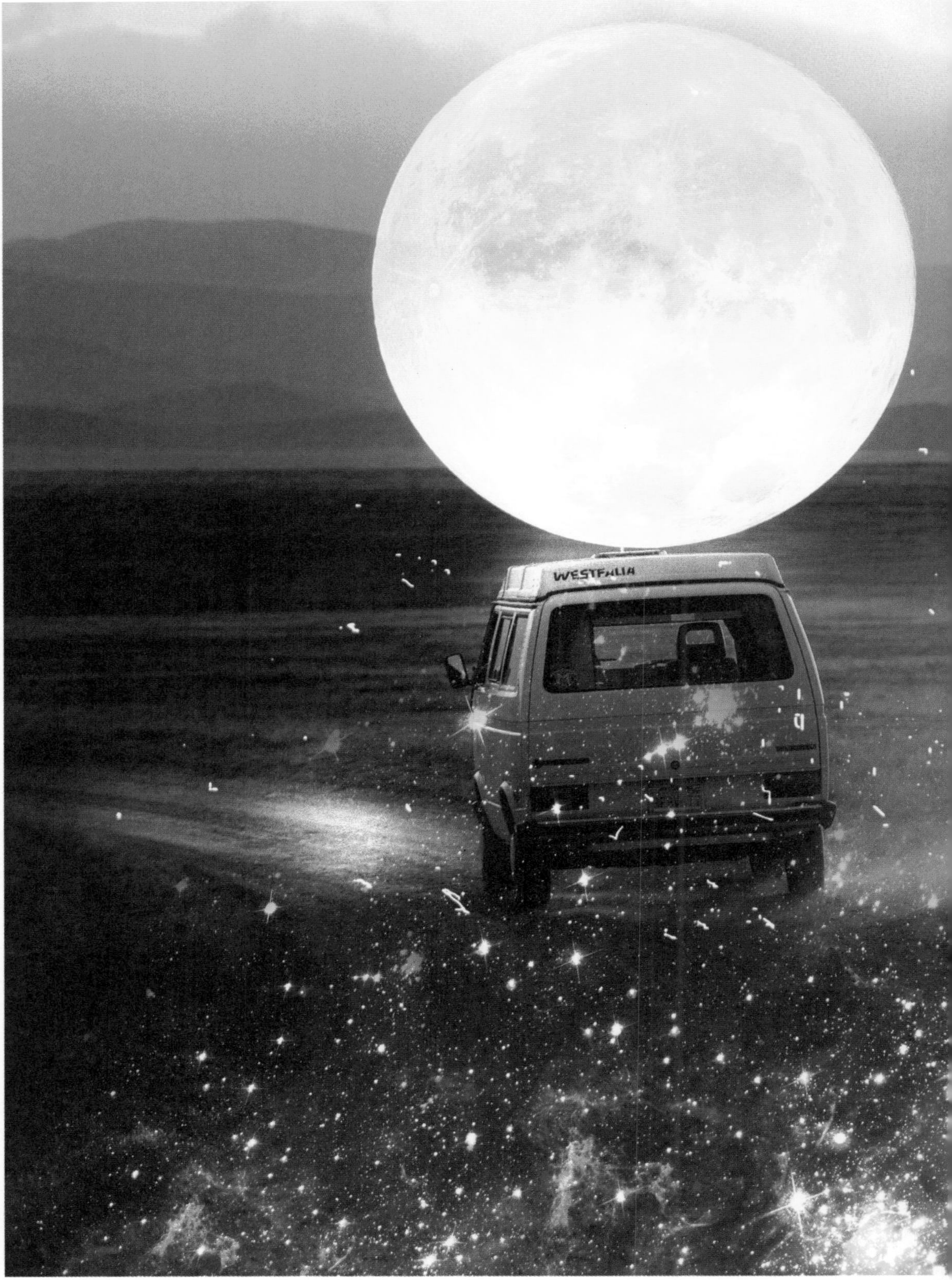
WESTFALIA

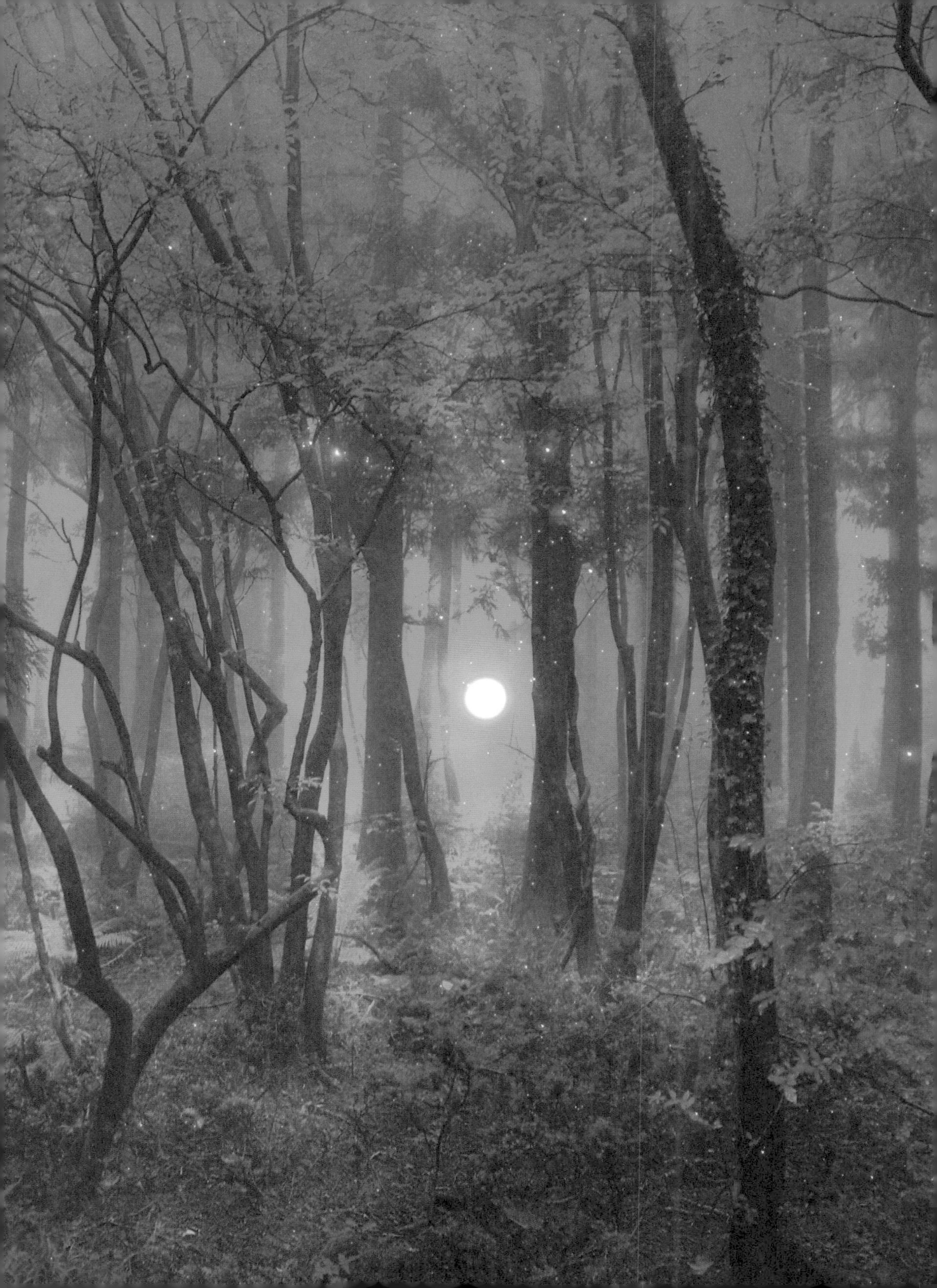

EARTH SIGNS These are Taurus, Virgo and Capricorn.

Boost Productivity

This moon fix is dedicated to those days of the month when the moon is shifting through the earth signs to help you tune in to the industrious and productive but also sensual energy associated with this element. Earth is rich, solid and generous. It nourishes, sustains and protects us. Although earth keeps our feet firmly on the ground to the point of stubbornly slowing us down at times, it can also be the element to ground us and take care of us.

YOU WILL NEED

- Tree
- Apple

METHOD

1. Seek out a tree in your garden or local park and study it.
2. Lean against that tree. Touch it, feel its texture.
3. Close your eyes and visualize yourself as a tree. Feel your roots growing strong in the earth.
4. Still leaning against the tree, eat your apple mindfully.
5. Feel your connection to the tree, the ground, the wind, the sun, the moon, the light and the sky.
6. When you are ready, thank the tree for allowing you to connect in this way as you feel the grounded, nourishing strength of that tree boosting your energy and productivity.

WATER SIGNS These are Cancer, Scorpio and Pisces.

Ignite Your Intuition

Intuition is is the part of you that is separate from your thoughts. It is the part of you that the moon always talks to. This intuition-igniting moon fix is dedicated to those days of the month when the moon is drifting through the water signs to help you tune in to the sensitive, imaginative and intuitive energy associated with this element.

YOU WILL NEED

- A quiet space
- Glass of moon water (see method, page 89)
- Timer
- Pen
- Paper

METHOD

1. Find somewhere that you know you won't be disturbed.
2. Hold your glass of moon water in your hand. Study the water through the glass and see what is reflected in it.
3. Drink the water slowly, putting the glass down between sips. Avoid gulping. Set a timer for two minutes.
4. Sit down, close your eyes, be still and just breathe.
5. Let your thoughts flow for the next two minutes. Don't avoid or push them away. Just be. Notice the difference between being and thinking.
6. When your time is up, open your eyes and stretch.
7. If you have any intuitive insights, note them and write them down.
8. Whether or not you had any insights, congratulate yourself on taking some much-needed time away from the tyranny of your thoughts to find inner calm and to give your intuition an opportunity to surface.

REST AND REJUVENATION

The full moon is most often associated with rejuvenation but perhaps one of her most transformative phases is when we can barely see her at all. The new moon phase includes and is prefaced by the dark moon phase. Since ancient times this period of darkness has been regarded as a time for rest, silence and reflection, as well as internal growth.

The fixes in this section encourage you to release yourself from hardship and to move on, helped by a letting-go ritual, or to start your Monday off with positivity. They give give you time to reflect, as well as to take extra special care of your own needs and focus on what really matters to you.

FOR BEST RESULTS
Thursday is an adventurous
day to perform this ritual but it
can be performed on any day.

Achieve Your Goals

This waxing moon ritual is designed to wake you up after a period of rest
and reflection. It will help reenergize you and move you from dreaming
about what you want to achieve in your life to taking action on those goals.
The waxing moon's energy is perfect for looking at the bigger picture of
your life, visualizing your ideal future and setting intentions.

YOU WILL NEED

- Quiet space
- Moonstone crystal
- Notebook
- Coloured pens

METHOD

1 When the moon is waxing, sit somewhere where you won't be disturbed.
   Place your moonstone crystal nearby.
2 Open your notebook and record the time and date.
3 Say out loud the following affirmation: 'I open myself and my life up to
   receiving something positive for both myself and others.'
4 Then write down a list of your desires. You can stick to one or list several.
   For each desire write it in the colour that is most appropriate to that goal.
   See page 46 for the significance of the colours. As you write, make your
   list of intentions as beautiful to look at as possible.
5 Read your list of intentions and visualize each of them coming true.
6 When you have finished, tear the paper out of the notebook and put your
   list of intentions somewhere you are going to see it every day. Place your
   moonstone crystal over your intentions to help focus your energy.

Sunday Reflection

Sunday is typically considered a day of rest and renewal. As its name suggests, Sunday is associated with the energy of the sun. Your sun sign represents the image you have of yourself, who you want to be and how others regard you. Each sun sign is believed to have its own personality traits and potential. Whether or not you subscribe to or believe in astrology, use the affirmations for each sun sign opposite as a starting point to boost your creativity and help you understand yourself better, to discover what truly fulfils you.

YOU WILL NEED

- Notepaper
- Pen
- Mantra

METHOD

1   When you get up on Sunday morning, write down the corresponding mantra for your sun sign (see opposite) on a piece of paper three times.
2   Say your mantra out loud three times. Commit the mantra to memory.
3   Write down at least three different ways you can embody that mantra.
4   Before you go to bed look at or visualize the moon and say the mantra out loud and visualize yourself living that mantra.

ENHANCE YOUR MOON WORK

Connect with the energy and symbolism of your birth or sun sign on any Sunday in the lunar cycle and use that energy to help you focus on what really matters to you.

SUN SIGN	BIRTH DATES	MANTRA
Aquarius	20 January to 18 February	I express original ideas
Pisces	19 February to 20 March	I see beneath the surface of things
Aries	21 March to 19 April	I am an inspiring force
Taurus	20 April to 20 May	I have the inner peace I need
Gemini	21 May to 20 June	I bring variety to the universe
Cancer	21 June to 22 July	I nurture both myself and others
Leo	23 July to 22 August	I inspire others with my inner joy
Virgo	23 August to 22 September	My energy is productive and healing
Libra	23 September to 22 October	I embody harmony and peace
Scorpio	23 October to 21 November	I renew myself and inspire others
Sagittarius	22 November to 21 December	I thrive when I am challenged
Capricorn	22 December to 19 January	I am a source of wisdom

FOR BEST RESULTS Plan for a minimum of one hour of alone time to feel the effects.

Take Time to Reenergize

Take some time out of your normal routine to be by yourself when the moon is dark and taking her own time out. This fix is your time to simply be.

YOU WILL NEED

- Diary
- A pleasurable excursion
- Moon journal (see page 39)
- Pen

METHOD

1. Find out when the moon is going to be in a dark or new phase and mark down in your diary a day or period of time when you can be completely alone. If you have children, you will need to organize care in advance for them.
2. Tell people you will be unreachable unless it's an absolute emergency. They will understand your need for some 'me time'.
3. Stick to that schedule.
4. When the day comes, switch off your phone, making sure only your nearest and dearest can reach you in the unlikely case there is a real emergency.
5. Then take your time out doing something that enriches you in a positive way. It could be a trip to the cinema or a museum, a meal alone in a restaurant with a good book, or a trip to a spa. The important thing is that you break your normal routine and treat yourself to the pleasure of your own company, so you can come back refreshed and rejuvenated. If at any point you feel guilty, remind yourself that the moon is also taking time right now to rest and rejuvenate.
6. At the end of the day write down how it made you feel in your moon journal.

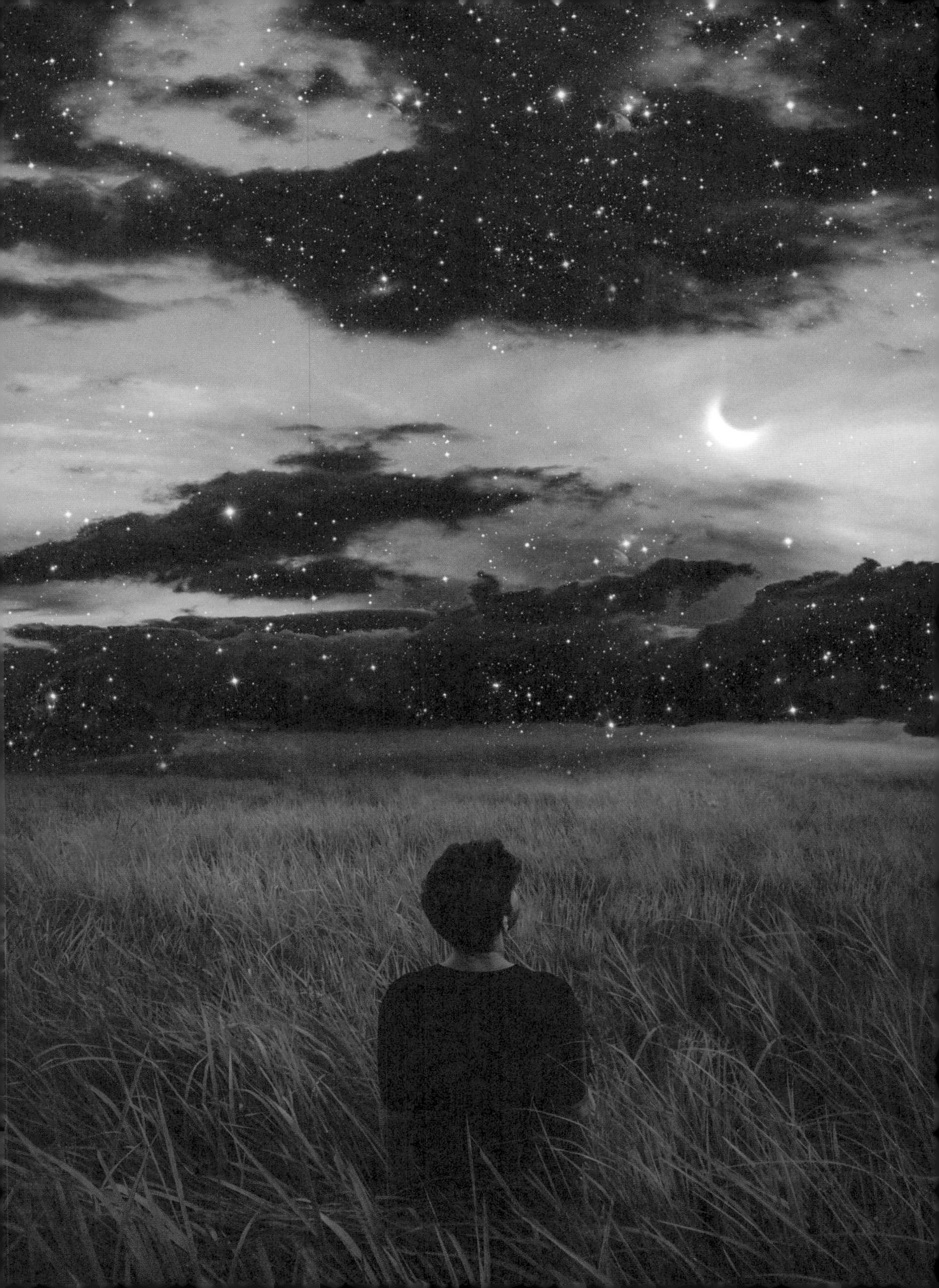

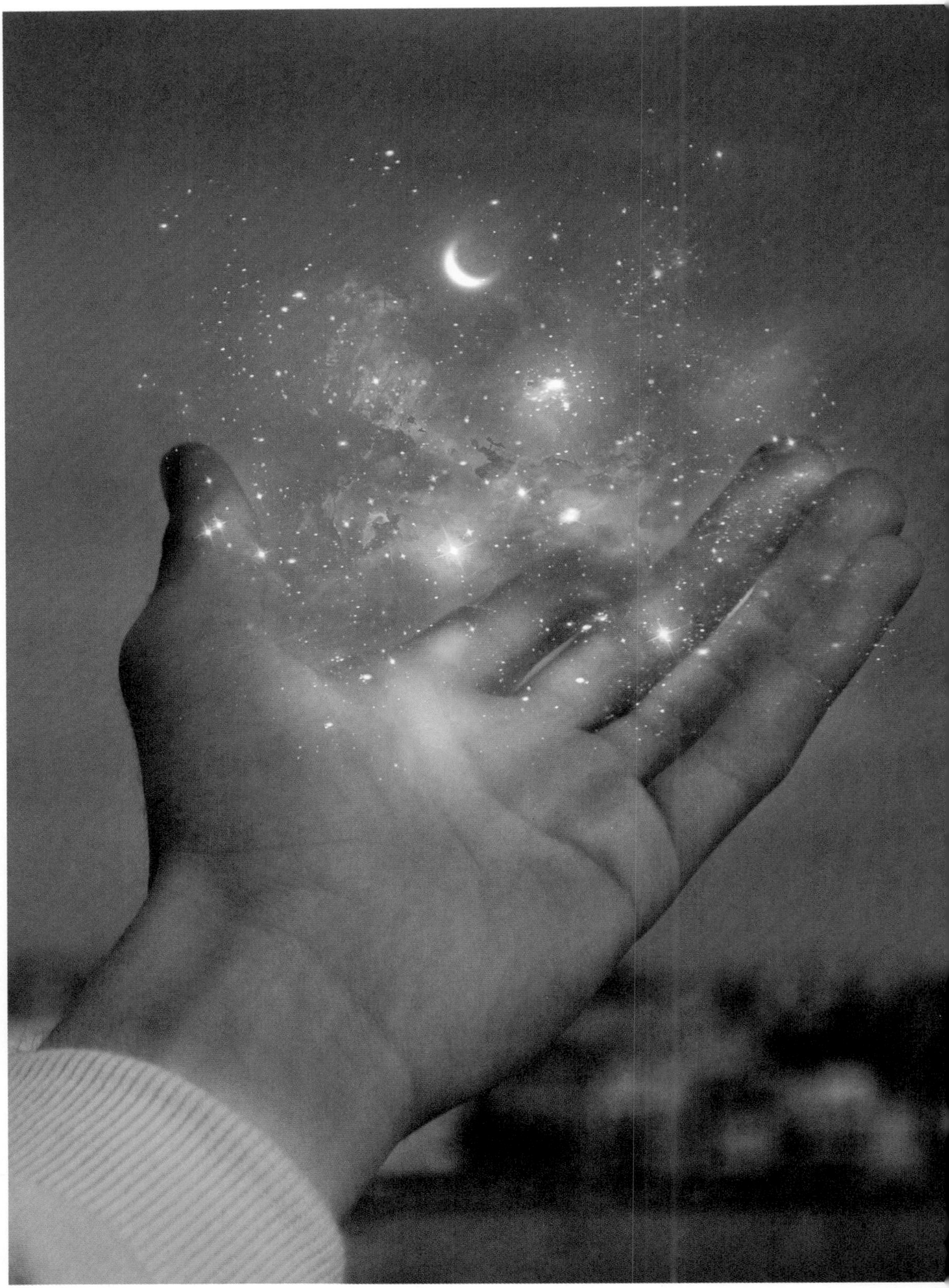

FOR BEST RESULTS The ideal day to perform this is on a Friday as this is the day associated with love and forgiveness, both of yourself and others.

Letting-Go Ritual

This moon fix should be performed when the moon is either waning or not visible as this is when she is shedding her light. The quiet and reflective lunar energy offers an amazing opportunity to lovingly let go of people and things that were once central to our identity – for example when a relationship ends, we change careers, or a close friendship just fades from our lives. Many of us struggle to come to terms with goodbyes and shedding roles we have once had.

YOU WILL NEED
- A twig or a leaf (or balloon)
- Source of natural running water

METHOD
1 Think of someone who or something that you need to let go of in your life. It could be a relationship or a stage in your life that you have moved away from.
2 When the moon is waning or dark, head outside, go find a leaf or a small twig. Study the details of that leaf or twig.
3 Visualize that twig or leaf as your past identity.
4 Take it to a nearby stream, river or other source of natural running water. Mindfully drop it in and watch it and your past self drift away.
5 If you can't find a source of running water you can do this ritual with a small balloon that you release into the air and watch float away.

VIOLET LOTUS This is associated with the crown chakra in Hindu and yogic traditions. The crown chakra is the area on top of your head and is associated with renewal and spiritual transformation.

Encourage Spiritual Growth

The colours in your life have a powerful impact on you psychologically and emotionally. Perhaps the most relaxing and empowering colour is that most strongly associated with spiritual growth and releasing feelings of sadness – the colour purple, violet, in particular. This moon fix should be performed when the moon is waning and lunar energy is encouraging you to be more reflective, rather than proactive.

YOU WILL NEED

- Picture of a lotus flower
- Purple pens/computer font
- Violet essential oil
- Purple items of jewellery or clothing
- Purple candles
- Matches/lighter

METHOD

1. Search for a picture of a violet lotus flower, print it out and put it on your wall or make it your screen saver.
2. When writing, use purple pens or type in purple font.
3. Rub a few drops of violet essential oil on your hands.
4. Wear purple items of clothes or jewellery during this time.
5. Light purple candles and visualize healing violet light surrounding you and radiating from the top of your head.
6. Open your eyes, heart and life to the colour purple and allow this healing colour to heal emotional wounds and open up a connection between your heart and the wise and peaceful part of you.

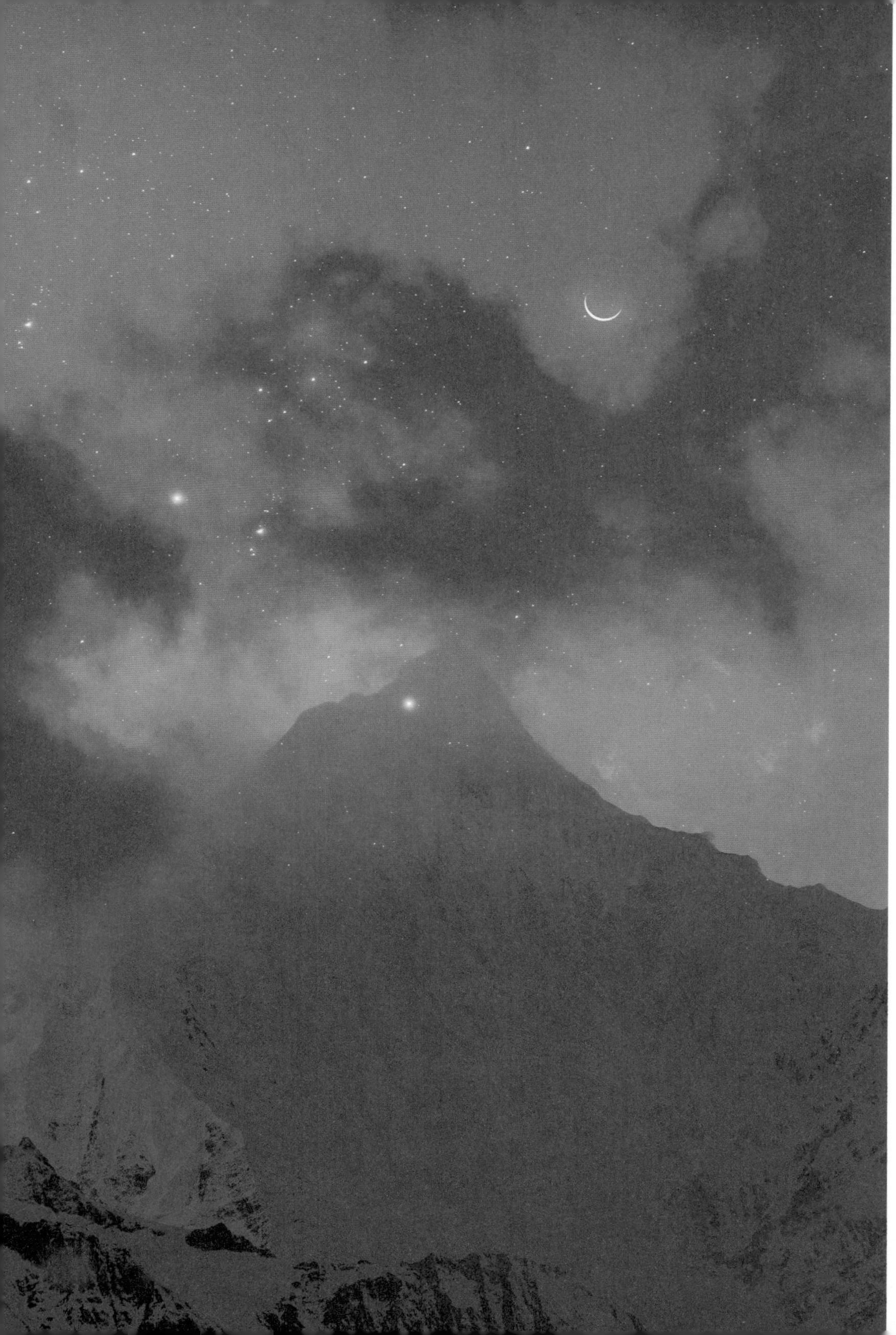

FOR BEST RESULTS
Perform this ritual on a
Tuesday, the day ruled by
Mars, the planet of action.

Boost Your Mood

This moon fix draws on the power of music to motivate. Studies show that music plays a beneficial role in easing stress, increasing focus and boosting mood and motivation. It should be performed when the moon is waxing because just as the moon is increasing in the sky this fix will inspire you to take action on realizing your intentions.

YOU WILL NEED

- Your coloured list of intentions (see method, page 125)
- Pen
- Headphones
- Energizing music

METHOD

1   Every day, when the moon is waxing, before you head to work or your day begins in earnest, review your coloured list of intentions. Tick off items if you've completed them. Write down whatever you desire, whether small or big, because achieving even small goals empowers the flow of abundance into your life. Everything you do that makes you feel more happy builds momentum for you.

2   Put your headphones on and listen to your favourite piece of upbeat music for a few minutes. The song must be energizing and make you want to tap your feet or sing.

3   Transform listening to your song into a motivational waxing moon ritual by focusing on nothing but that song. Hear and feel the good sound vibes. You can listen to a different upbeat song each day or the same track if it always acts to energize you to get moving and start living the life of your big dreams.

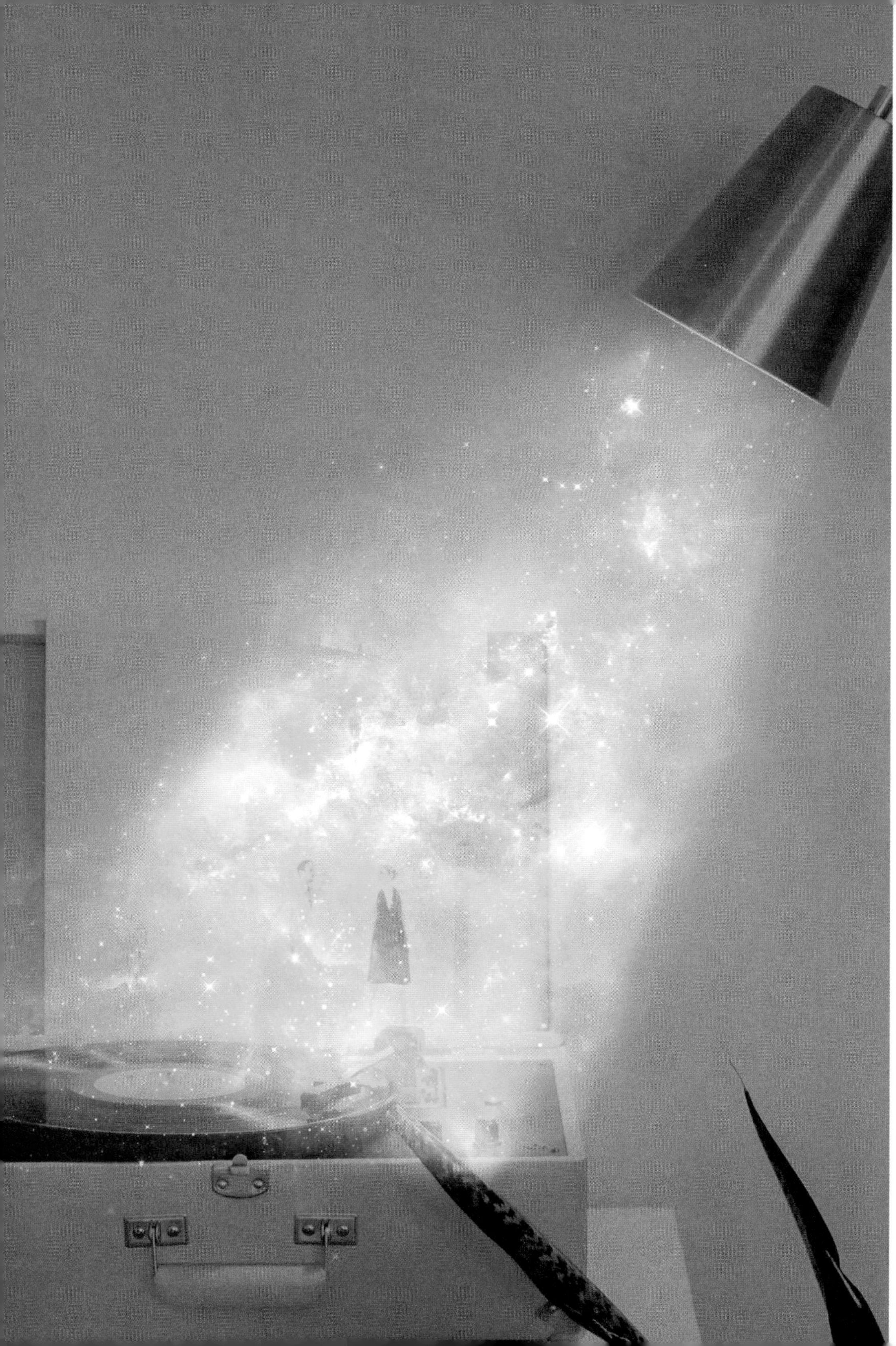

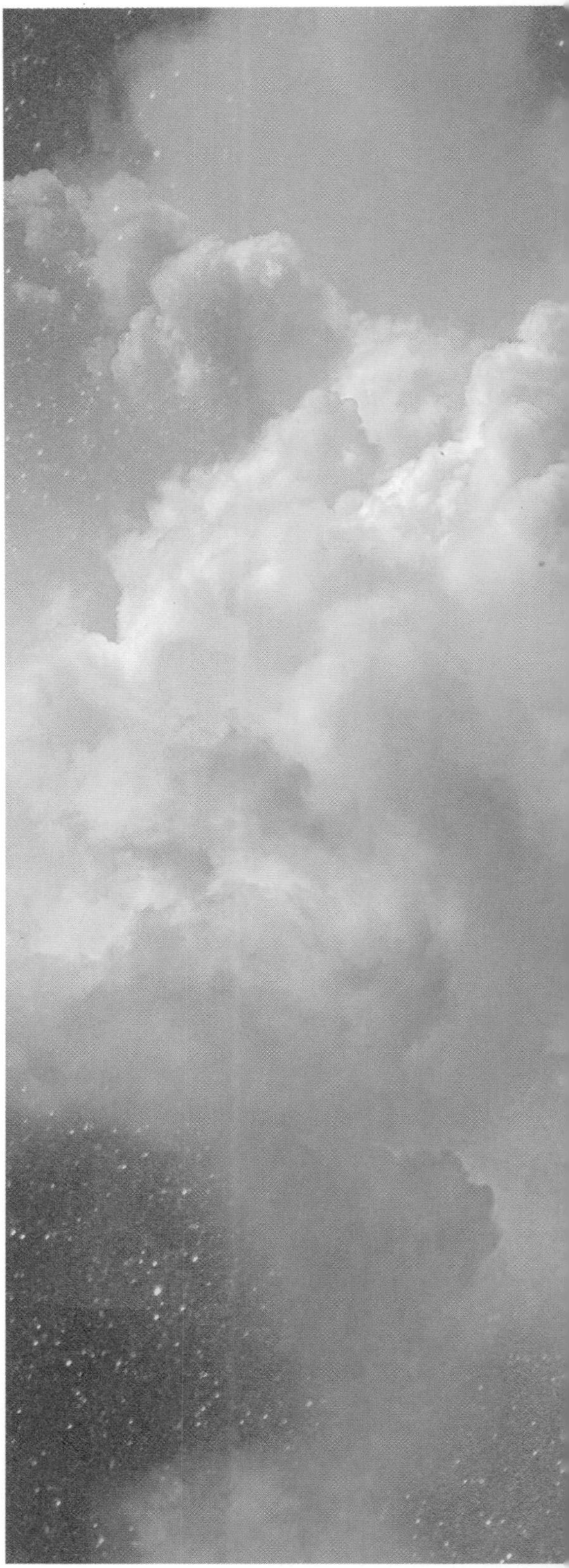

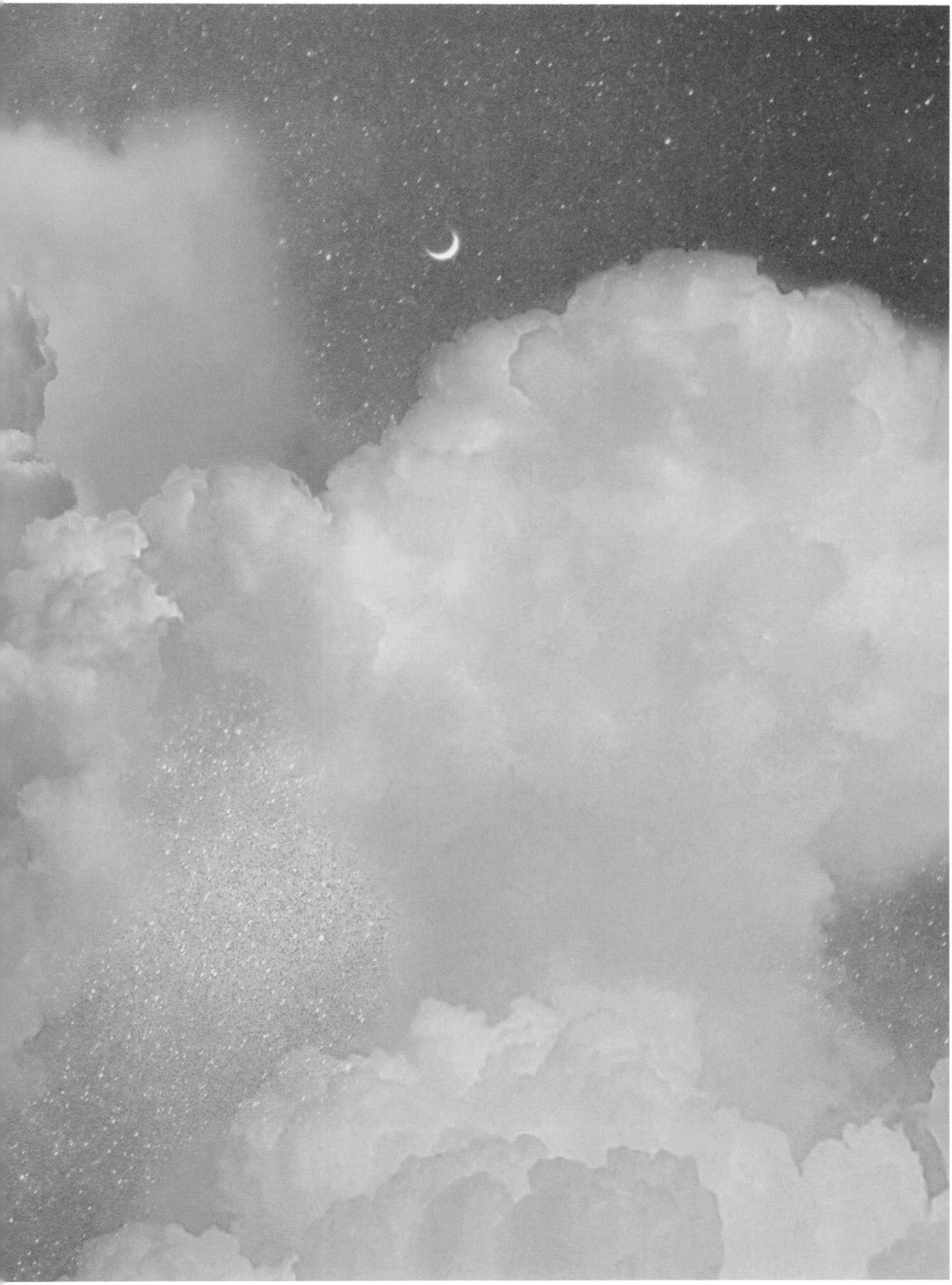

FOR BEST RESULTS
Perform on one day or in stages over several days when the moon is full.

Full Moon Rejuvenation

The full moon is a time when the moon's energy is at its largest and brightest. You may notice your energies and emotions can become more heightened than normal. This moon fix encourages you to consciously align yourself completely with the cleansing, releasing and rejuvenating intensity and power of the full moon.

YOU WILL NEED

- Bergamot incense sticks
- Matches/lighter
- Face mask
- Epsom salts
- Moonstone or clear quartz crystals
- Your list of intentions (see method, page 125)

METHOD

1 When the moon is full, tidy your bedroom and remove all clutter.
2 Burn recharging bergamot incense sticks and ensure your living space is filled with heavenly natural aromas.
3 Treat yourself to a face mask.
4 Use Epsom salts in your bath to cleanse and detoxify.
5 Charge your crystals under the light of the moon (see page 45).
6 Indulge in a spot of moon bathing (see page 48) and as you do, spend time congratulating yourself for any progress made. If things haven't gone to plan, reflect on this as something you can learn and grow from.
7 Rewrite your list of intentions, revising them according to any progress made.

Bring Positivity to Mondays

Monday often has negative associations given that it is the start of the working week after the relaxation of the weekend, but, hopefully, this ritual will help you see every Monday from now on in an illuminating new light. As its name suggests, Monday is associated with the enchantment of the moon. The moon reflects the light of the sun. In astrology, your moon sign is believed to represent your emotions or the real or true inner you, whereas your sun sign represents the external or the image you present to the world. This makes Monday the perfect day to reflect on yourself and your emotional needs.

FOR BEST RESULTS This moon fix can be performed on any Monday in the lunar cycle.

YOU WILL NEED

- Glass of moon water (see method, page 89)
- White, silver or pale blue clothing or jewellery
- Moonstone crystal
- Natural water setting
- Swimwear
- Diary/moon journal (see page 39)
- Pen

METHOD

1 Begin your Monday by drinking a full glass of moon water.
2 Say this affirmation out loud before you eat breakfast: 'Monday is the day of the moon. I am grateful for this magical day and the inspiration it will bring into my life.'
3 Wear white, silver or pale blue items of clothing or jewellery.
4 Carry your moonstone crystal with you.
5 Make self-care and finding balance in your life your focus today. If you have been very sociable recently, plan some time alone. If you have been preoccupied, plan to spend time with loved ones.
6 At some point in the day, be sure to check what phase the moon is currently in and perform a mini moon meditation (see page 40).
7 Notice the element of water during the day, whenever you drink, wash or clean. Each time give thanks for water energy and the boost it gives to your intuition and creativity.
8 Go swimming or walk beside a river, lake or the seaside if you can.
9 Make planning a priority today if you can. Tuesday is a better day for the action to begin.
10 Find things to be grateful for today.
11 Write down how you feel in a journal.
12 End your day by giving thanks to the moon for all the good things in your life.

PROTECTION AND COMFORT

The moon goddess is the archetype of the sacred feminine with all her ancient associations with unconditional love, protection and comfort. In this section, you will find moon fixes to awaken feelings of unconditional love for yourself and others, so you can more easily tune in to your inner wisdom and make better decisions whenever you feel vulnerable or are making decisions which aren't in your best or highest interests. There are also fixes to help you detox negative influences from your life and to help ease feelings of anxiety and fear which you can replace with soothing feelings of comfort and safety.

GREEK GODDESS ARTEMIS This huntress was responsible for maidens, chastity and also childbirth.

Invite Courage from the Maiden Goddess

Find inspiration, courage and fresh new beginnings by meditating on wise Artemis. The new and waxing moon phases correspond to the moon goddess in her guise as the maiden. The new moon in particular is believed to be the optimum time to plant seeds, plan ahead, and set goals and intentions for the month ahead.

YOU WILL NEED

- A quiet, comfortable space, where you can sit
- Sage incense sticks
- Matches/lighter
- Picture of the goddess Artemis
- Moon journal
- Pen

METHOD

1 When the moon is new find somewhere quiet where you can sit comfortably.
2 Burn sage incense to clear any negative energy and for protection.
3 Study your picture of the goddess Artemis for as long as you want.
4 Say the name of the goddess Artemis out loud three times and open out your arms as if to welcome an invisible presence.
5 Drop your arms and close your eyes. Visualize the picture.
6 Silently ask Artemis for what you want to welcome into your life.
7 Sit quietly for at least five minutes and notice how your body feels. See if you can sense Artemis speaking to you through your feelings and what you sense in your body.
8 When you have finished write down what you sensed in your moon journal (see page 39).

GREEK GODDESS SELENE She was said
to drive her silver chariot, drawn by winged
white horses, across the night sky, plunging
into the sea as day breaks.

Find Nurture from the Mother Goddess

This moon fix meditation is dedicated to the moon goddess Selene, who represents the mother aspect of the sacred feminine, and should be performed indoors when the moon is full. Use it to invite Selene's unconditional love and nurturing presence in your life.

YOU WILL NEED
- Phone/timer
- White candle
- Matches/lighter
- Picture of Selene

METHOD
1   When the moon is full, set an alarm for 30 minutes.
2   Sit comfortably and light a white candle, as a symbol of the moon's spiritual grace.
3   Study the picture of Selene.
4   Study the flame of the candle for a few minutes.
5   Close your eyes and breathe deeply. Say the name Selene out loud three times.
6   Visualize Selene with her arms open as if to embrace you.
7   Imagine that light is flowing from Selene's open arms towards you.
8   Visualize that light surrounding you completely.
9   Savour the feeling of unconditional love as Selene's light embraces you.
10 When you are ready, visualize Selene's light entering your heart and see her returning to the moon.
11 Open your eyes and focus your eyes on your picture of her, giving thanks for the gifts she has blessed you with. Then safely extinguish your candle.

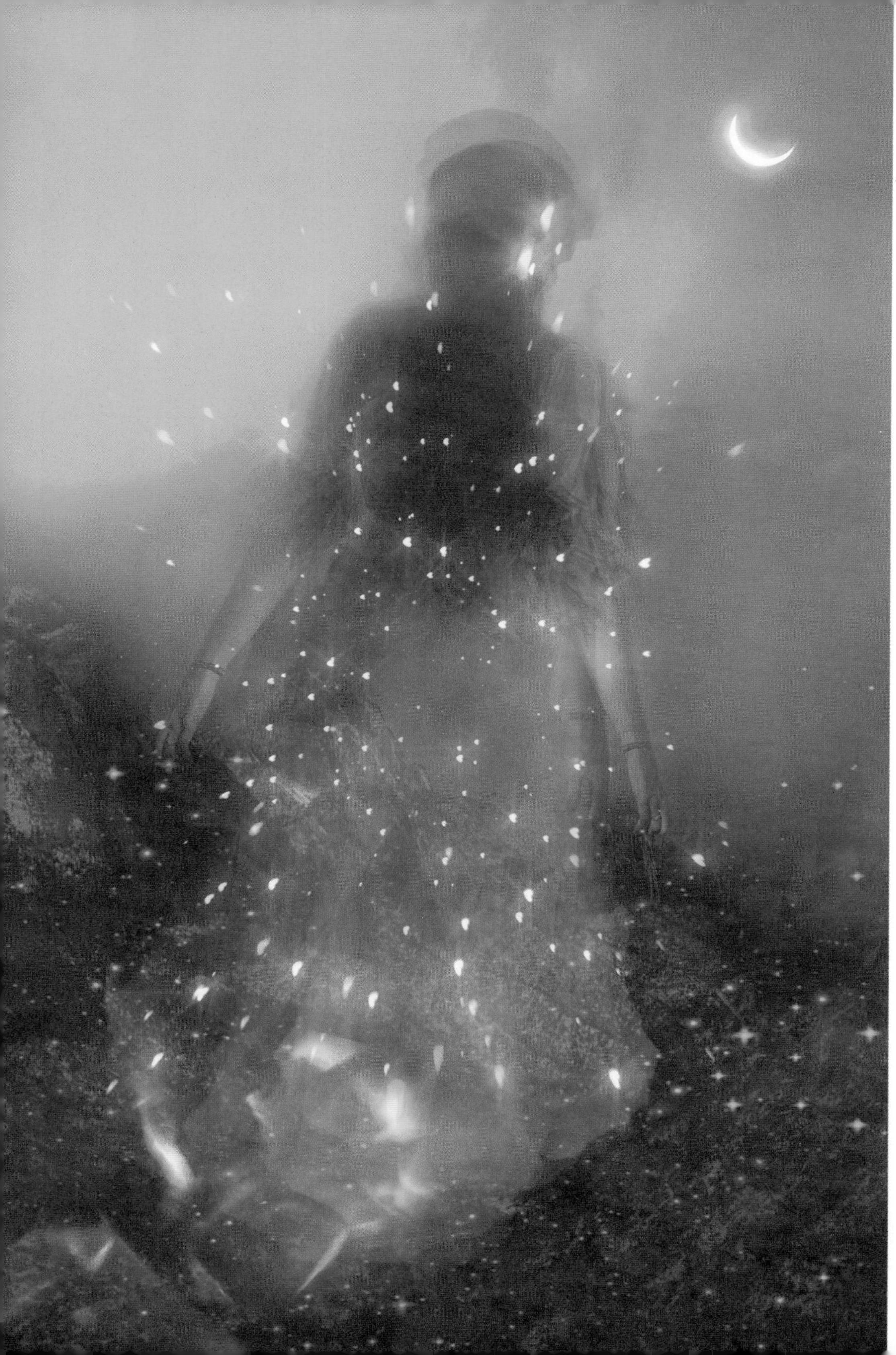

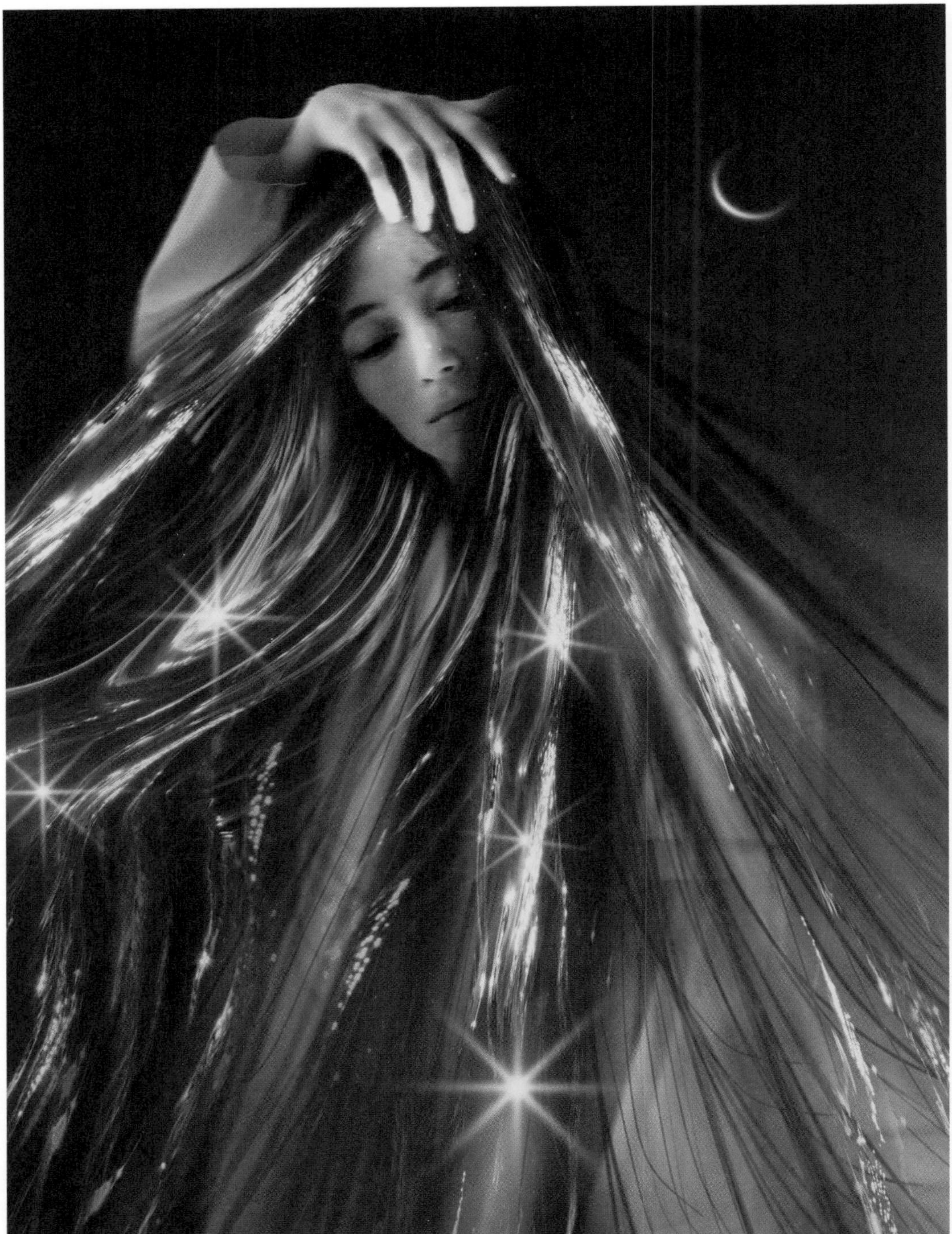

GREEK GODDESS HECATE Shrines to this protective deity were placed at the door of a family home in order to call down blessings upon those inside.

Seek Reflection from the Wise Woman

This outdoor moon meditation is dedicated to the wise and mystical moon goddess Hecate. It celebrates the reflective, mature and wise parts of ourselves, regardless of gender.

YOU WILL NEED

- Picture of Hecate
- Coat or shawl

METHOD

1. When the moon is waning or dark and unseen take a few moments in the evening when it is dark to study a picture of the moon goddess Hecate.
2. Put on a warm coat or shawl and step outside into your garden or drive.
3. Once outside, ensure you are safe and away from any passing traffic.
4. Take slow, deep breaths and visualize the picture of Hecate you have studied. Whisper her name three times.
5. Tune in to the atmosphere around you. Be aware of what you hear, see and feel.
6. Keeping your eyes open, imagine there are grey stones beneath your feet and standing beside you is Hecate.
7. Imagine Hecate placing her arm around you and resting your head on her shoulder. Visualize the grey stones you are standing on turning to silver.
8. Imagine Hecate telling you to notice every one of the silver stones beneath you. The light from those stones is so bright you can feel their power vibrating through you.
9. When you have absorbed the energy of the silver stones thank Hecate for her wisdom and grace. Imagine her floating away.
10. When Hecate has vanished from your mind's eye, take a deep breath, blink several times and bring your awareness back to the here and now.

ENHANCE YOUR MOON WORK
Be aware that your appetite is affected
by whether the moon's energy is increasing
or decreasing.

Banish Negative Cravings

Turning to food when you are in need of comfort is a recipe for unhappiness, weight gain and poor health. This moon fix encourages you to stop and reflect on which phase the moon is in whenever you get a food craving in order to determine whether you are really hungry or merely craving something food can never satisfy.

YOU WILL NEED
- Notebook
- Pen

METHOD

1   The next time you get a food craving between meals always pause for a moment between your craving and actually eating.
2   Write down the time and date and which foods you are craving.
3   Place your fist on your stomach, below the breastbone, and place all your awareness on that area. What do you feel? Emptiness or fullness?
4   Check what phase the moon is in. If the moon is new or waxing or full, ask yourself if you are hungry or just bored and in need of stimulation. If the moon is waning, its energy is decreasing, so question if you are tired or in need of support.
5   Take a 10-minute walk if you think you are bored. If you feel tired, take a 10-minute nap. If you feel in need of support, message a friend.
6   Check in with your hunger again and if you still feel hungry reach for a healthy snack. After you have eaten, note it down. Writing down your cravings is a great way to minimize them because knowing you have to record it makes it less likely you will want to eat unhealthily.

See page 150 for a waning moon recipe; and page 151 for a waxing and full moon recipe.

THE MOON FIX

148

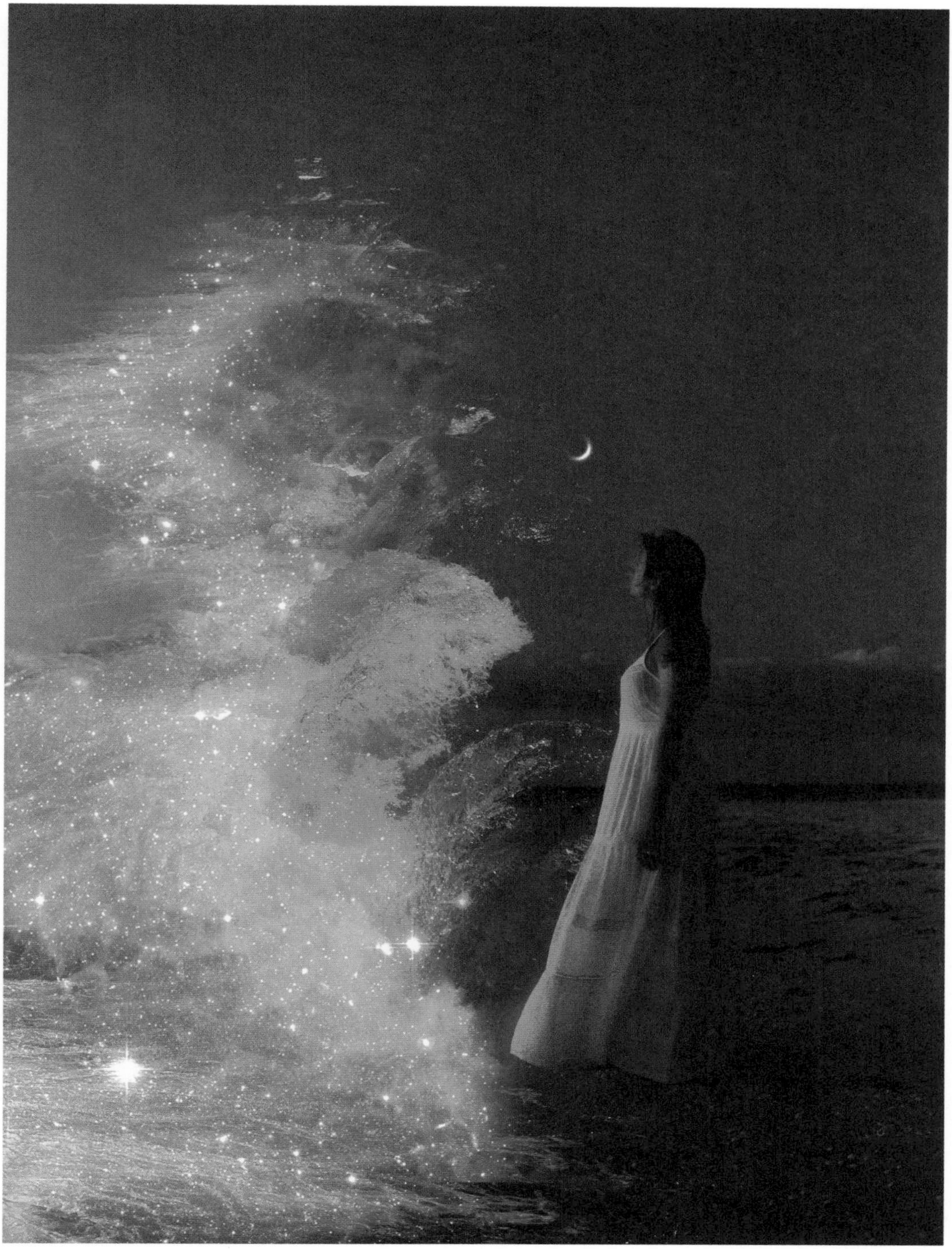

Butternut Squash and Sage Soup

SERVES 2–3

This wholesome and comforting soup is perfect for the waning moon period. The waning moon is all about letting go of what holds you back or what is toxic in your life and replacing what is bad for you with what is nourishing and healthy.

INGREDIENTS

- ½ tbsp olive oil
- ½ tbsp butter
- 1 onion, chopped
- 1 tbsp chopped sage
- 1 medium (approx. 1 kg/2 lb 4 oz) butternut squash, peeled, chopped and seeds removed
- 1 litre/1 quart vegetable stock
- chopped chives, to serve
- salt and black pepper, to taste
- plain breadsticks, to serve

METHOD

1   Melt the olive oil and butter in a pan over a medium heat.

2   Add the chopped onion and sage and cook gently for 10 minutes, or until the onions are soft.

3   Add the butternut squash and cook through for a few more minutes. Add the vegetable stock. Leave to simmer until the squash is soft and tender. Then mix with a stick blender until the soup is smooth. Add warm water, if it is too thick.

4   Reheat before serving, sprinkle with chopped chives and season with salt and black pepper to taste. Serve with the plain breadsticks.

Almond Cake

Almonds are believed to attract abundance and energy and during the waxing and full moon phases when lunar power is increasing, your moon fixes are all designed to help you attract good things into your life. They are a high-fat, nutrient-dense food and perfect for when the moon is increasing. If you cannot tolerate nuts, replace the almonds with sunflower seeds, which are also bursting with energy-boosting nutrients.

INGREDIENTS

- 115g/4 oz/1 stick butter
- 2 large eggs
- 115g/4 oz/1 cup plain/all-purpose flour
- 115g/4 oz/½ cup caster/superfine sugar
- 1 tsp baking powder
- 2 tsp vanilla extract
- 4–5 tbsp/20–25g sliced or flaked almonds
- icing/confectioners' sugar for dusting

METHOD

1 Preheat the oven to 180°C/350°F/Gas mark 4.

2 Lightly grease an 8-inch (20-cm) cake tin.

3 Melt the butter in a saucepan and allow to cool.

4 In a bowl, beat the eggs and then add the butter. Gradually add the flour, caster/superfine sugar, baking powder and vanilla extract, mixing until it's a smooth batter.

5 Pour the cake mixture into the cake tin, then sprinkle the sliced almonds over the top.

6 Bake for 25 minutes, or until golden brown. Place on a wire rack and allow to cool.

7 Dust with icing/confectioners' sugar to serve. Savour the delicious flavour under the light of the waxing or full moon when lunar power is growing and the time is perfect for focusing on what you want to increase or attract into your life.

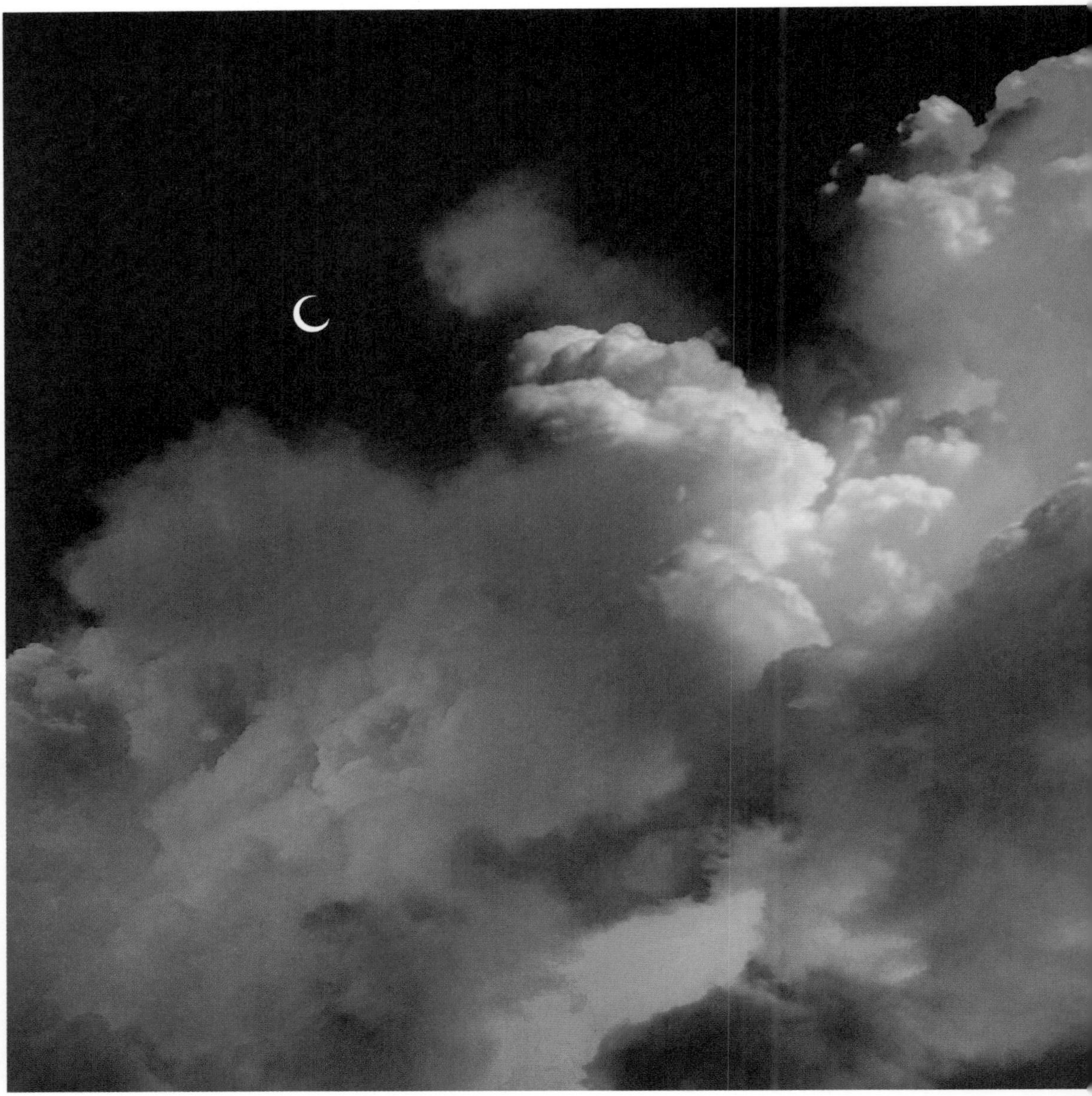

FOR BEST RESULTS The full moon offers the perfect opportunity to do a life detox.

Release Negative Energy

It's time to purge things in your life that are damaging your chances of success, health and happiness, such as an unhealthy diet, alcohol, smoking, toxic relationships or anxiety. This moon ritual can help you release negativity and protect yourself from self-sabotaging behaviour.

YOU WILL NEED

- Moon altar (see page 42)
- Jug of water
- Pieces of paper
- Pen
- White candle
- Matches/lighter
- Fireproof plate

METHOD

1   When the moon is full sit beside your moon altar with a filled jug of water.
2   Write down on small pieces of paper negative things or people you want to release from your life or negative things you need protecting from.
3   Light a candle.
4   Take one piece of paper and read it aloud. Reflect on what this person or thing you want to release has taught you about yourself. Remind yourself that failure, disappointment and making mistakes are all lessons that can help you learn and grow and evolve into a higher version of yourself.
5   Then dip the piece of paper into the candle gently so it starts to burn. Put it on the fireproof plate and watch it crumple and burn. Once it is in ashes, say 'Banished' or 'Be Gone'. Pour water over the ashes.
6   Repeat with the other pieces of paper.
7   When you are finished, give thanks to the full moon for her healing wisdom and safely extinguish your candle.

ENHANCE YOUR MOON WORK Using lavender regularly can induce a state of inner calm that will help you tune out negativity and tune in to the loving comfort and the protection of the moon.

Ablutions for Protection

This moon fix will help ease fear and anxiety and repel negative energy from invading your life. It can be performed on any day of the lunar cycle and is particularly beneficial when you feel vulnerable and unsupported.

YOU WILL NEED

- Moon altar (see page 42)
- Sage incense sticks
- Matches/lighter
- Bath
- Lavender essential oil, plus carrier oil
- Candles
- Calming music (optional)

METHOD

1. In the hour before you go to bed burn some sage incense sticks, preferably beside your moon altar.
2. Mentally express gratitude for the moon's healing presence in your life.
3. Visualize the light of the moon forming a protective bubble around you.
4. Say out loud, 'I am safe and protected by the arms of mother moon.'
5. Run a warm bath and add a few drops of lavender oil. Light some candles or play some calming music, then relax in the bath.
6. After your bath, mix a few drops of lavender oil with a carrier oil, such as almond or jojoba, and spritz your pillow or clothing.
7. In the coming days, when you feel in need of support and protection visualize the light of the moon forming a protective bubble around you.

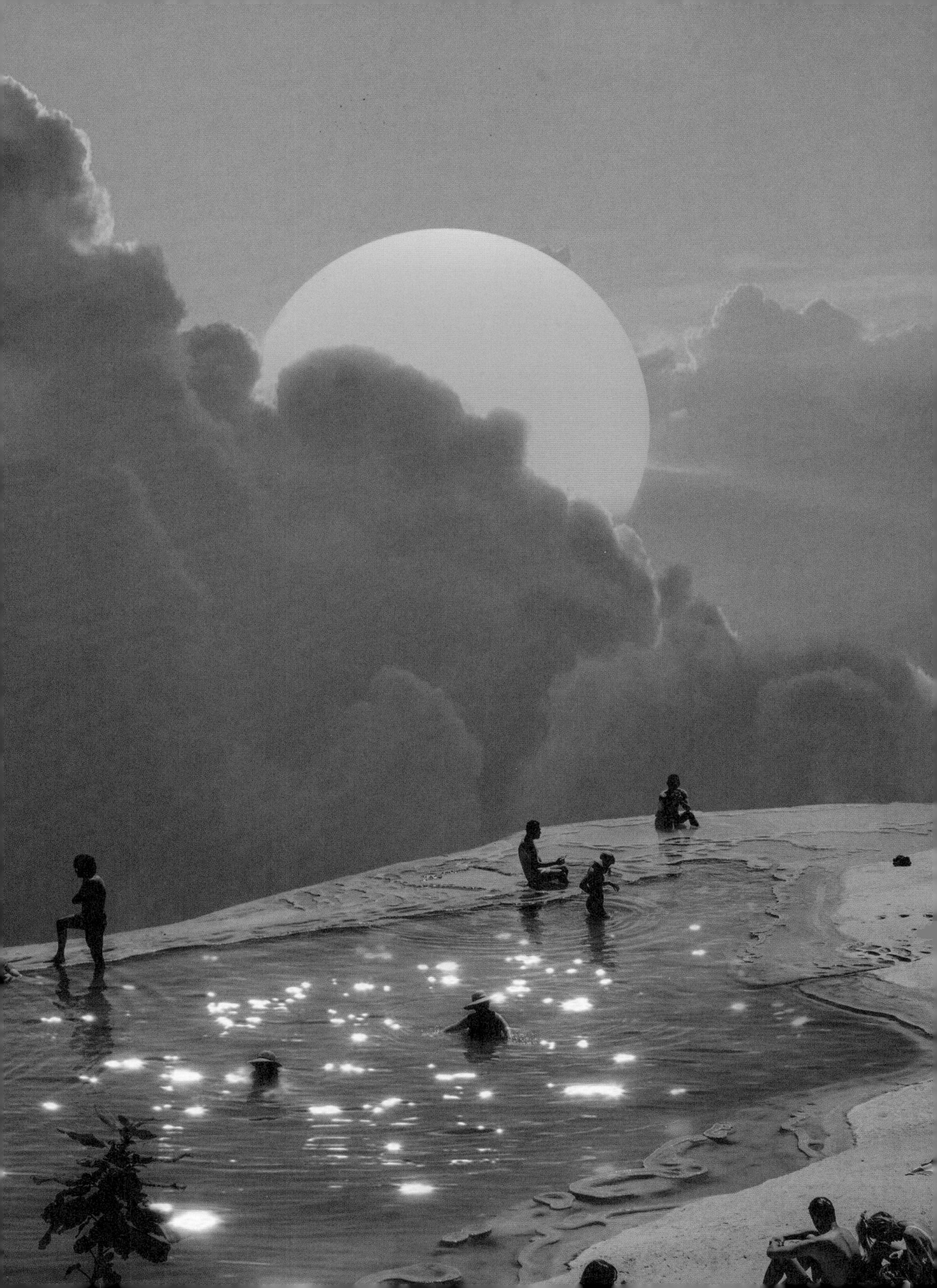

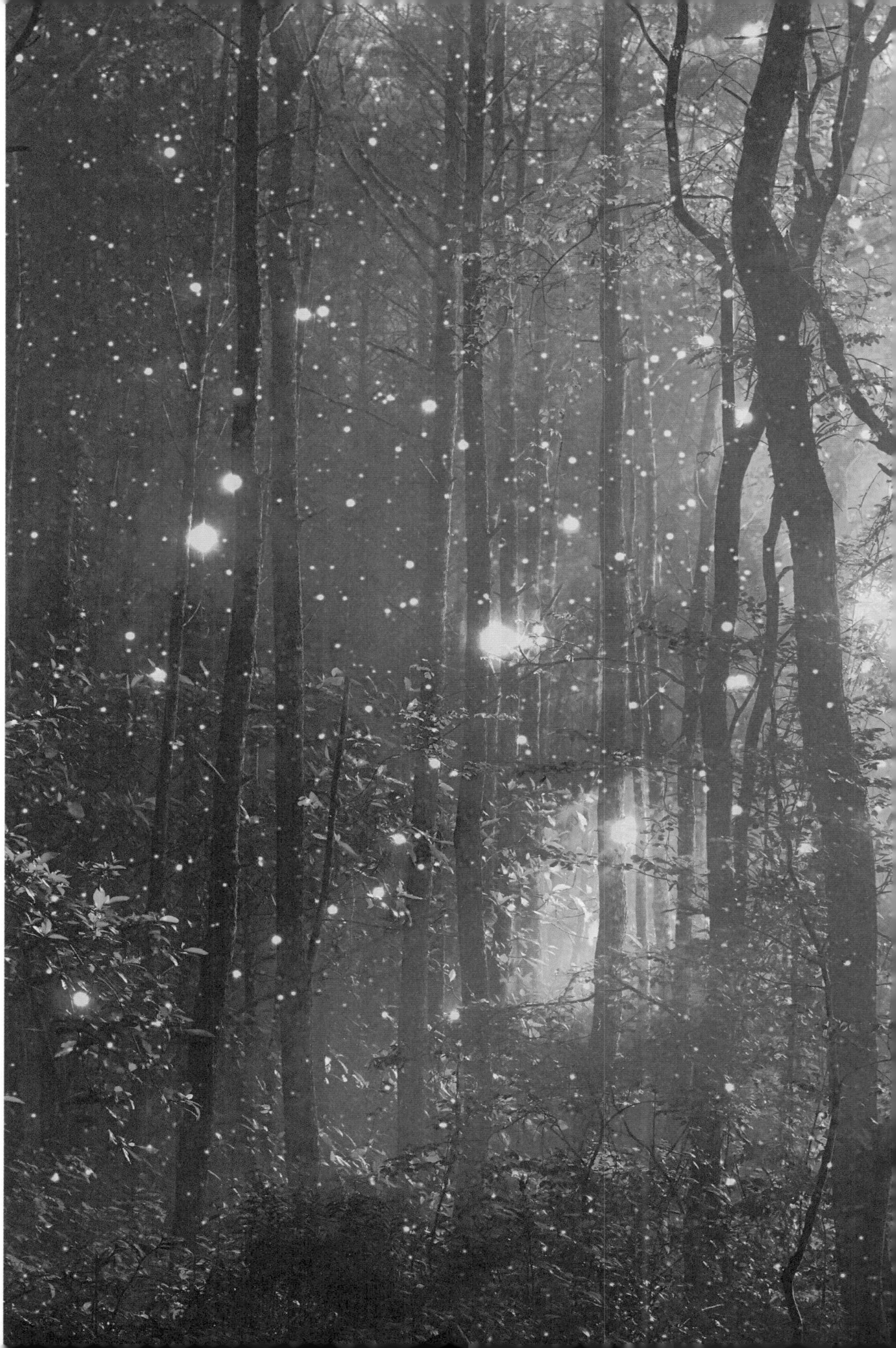

ENHANCE YOUR MOON WORK

The new moon invites new beginnings; taking action towards fulfilling your desires aligns with the energies of the waning moon; the full moon is a time of heightened creativity; and the waning moon favours completion, rest and reflection.

Find Harmony

Tuning in to the energies of the moon and understanding what activities, rituals and moon fixes are best suited to those energies can bring a sense of rhythm, healing and harmony into your life where it may have been lacking before. Whenever you feel in need of comfort and guidance, you can always tune in to the moon and draw down her loving protection and inspiration. This can be particularly reassuring when you feel more vulnerable than usual or when things in your life feel like they are spinning out of your control.

YOU WILL NEED

- Picture of the moon
- Notebook
- Pen

METHOD

1. On any day of the lunar month, except when the moon is dark and hidden from view, find out which specific phase the moon is in.
2. Search online to find a picture of that specific moon phase.
3. In your notebook, write down the date and time and draw that moon phase as best you can.
4. Use the information about the energies associated with phases of the moon on page 16 and write down how you feel the different energies and associations of that phase have impacted you or could impact you.

DREAM CATCHERS Typically, a dream catcher is round with a loop and threading that looks like a spider's web. There are also feathers and beads attached to the bottom. You can buy one, or see page 173 for a website that teaches you how to make your own.

Protection from Nightmares

The moon rules the land of sleep and dreams, but if you have unpleasant dreams this can cause considerable anxiety. This moon fix encourages you to use a dream catcher to ensure that your dreams are as healing and empowering as possible. There is a school of thought which believes that dreams reflect your state of mind, and if your dreams are empowering this can cross over into your waking life. In other words, the more positive and creative your dreams the more positive and inspiring your waking life can be.

YOU WILL NEED
- Dream catcher
- Sage incense

METHOD

1. The night air is filled with dreams both positive and negative, so when it is dark and the moon is out, hang a dream catcher over your bed, or place it close beside your bed.

2. Initiate your dream catcher the first time by burning some sage incense.

3. Then each night before you go to sleep, blow gently on it to bless it and say the following prayer: 'Dream catcher, bless my dreams with peace and joy.'

4. Ask the moon to send you through your dream catcher only the sweetest of dreams.

5. Bad dreams will get trapped in the spider's web part of the dream catcher. When morning comes they will meet the sunlight and be destroyed.

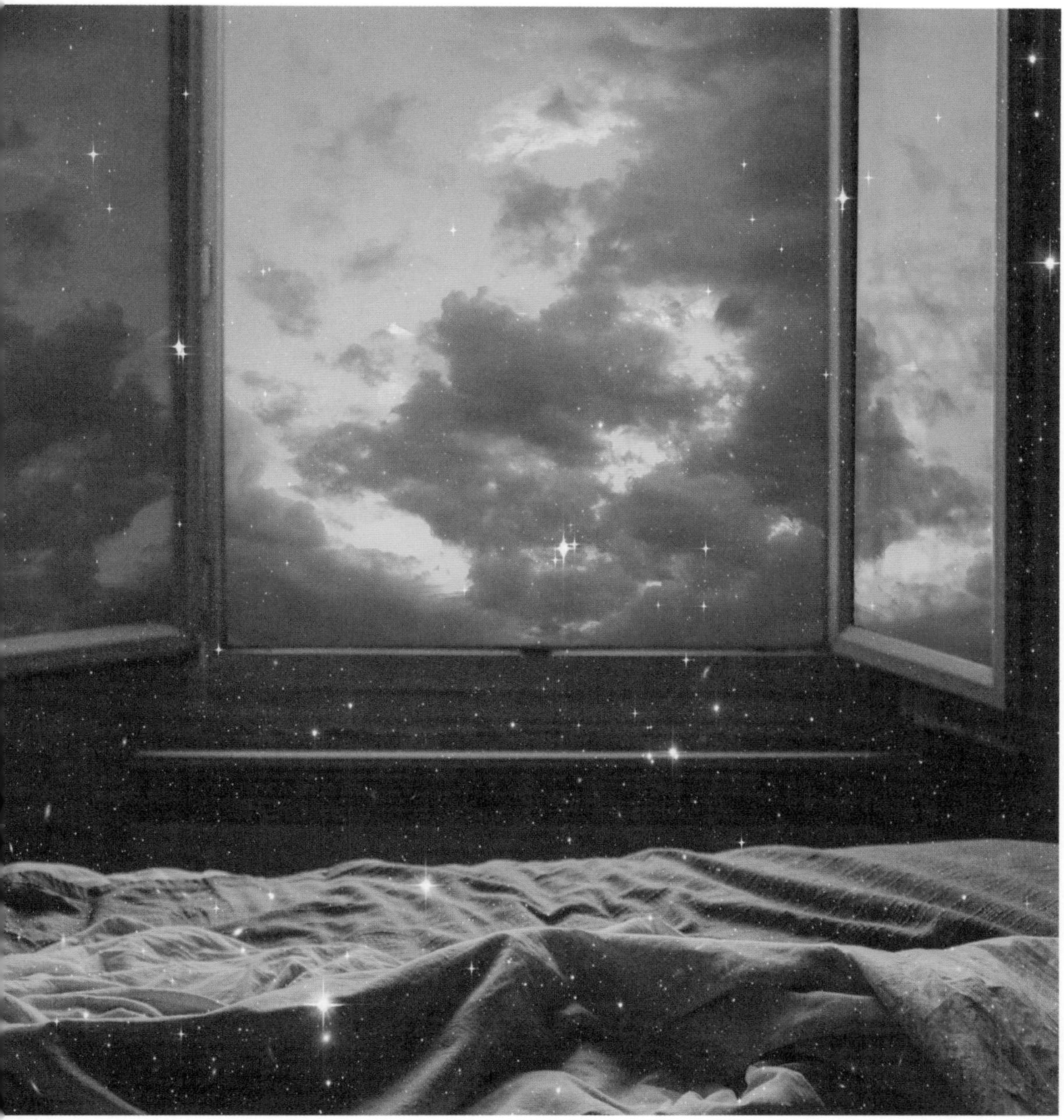

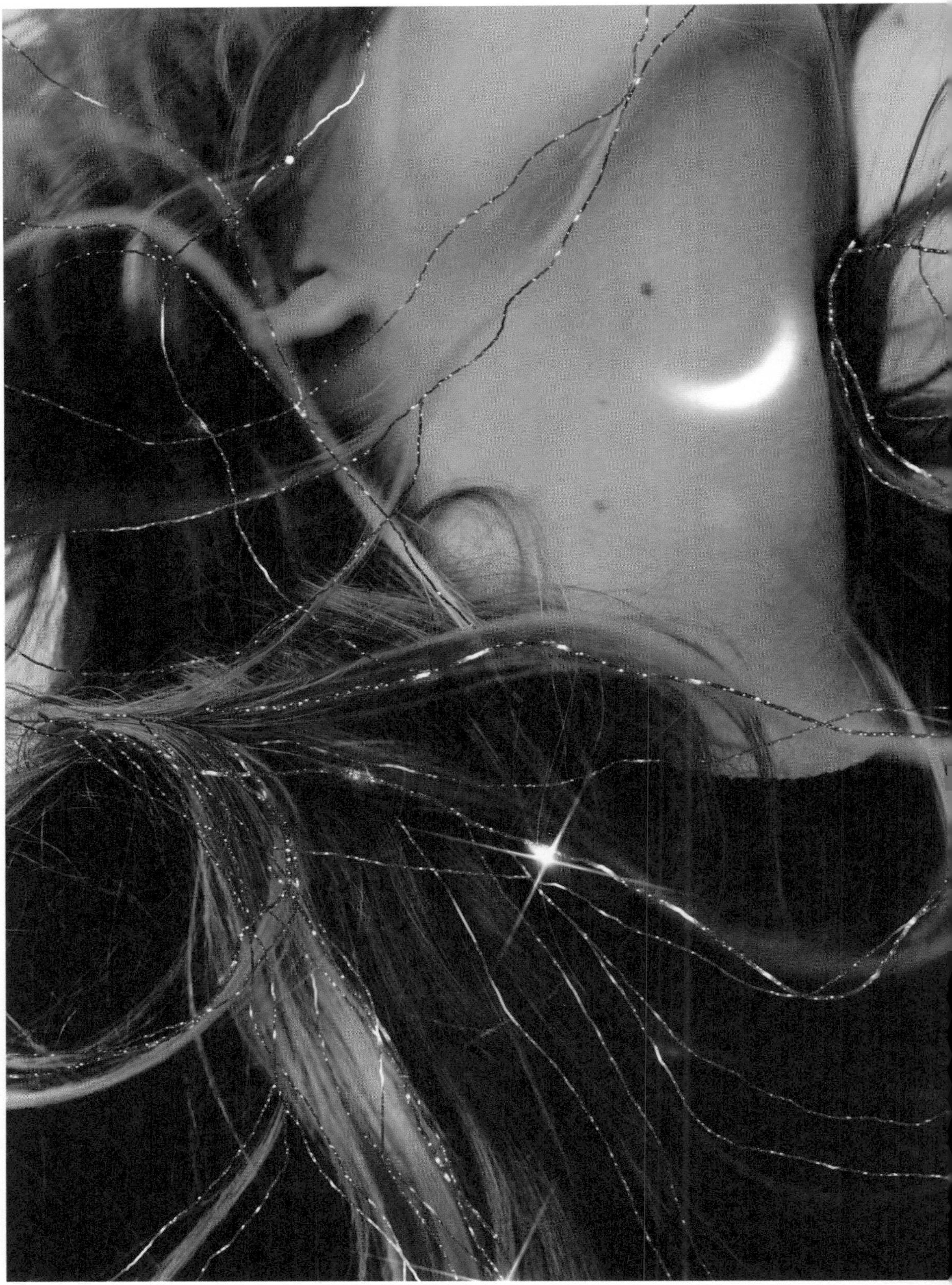

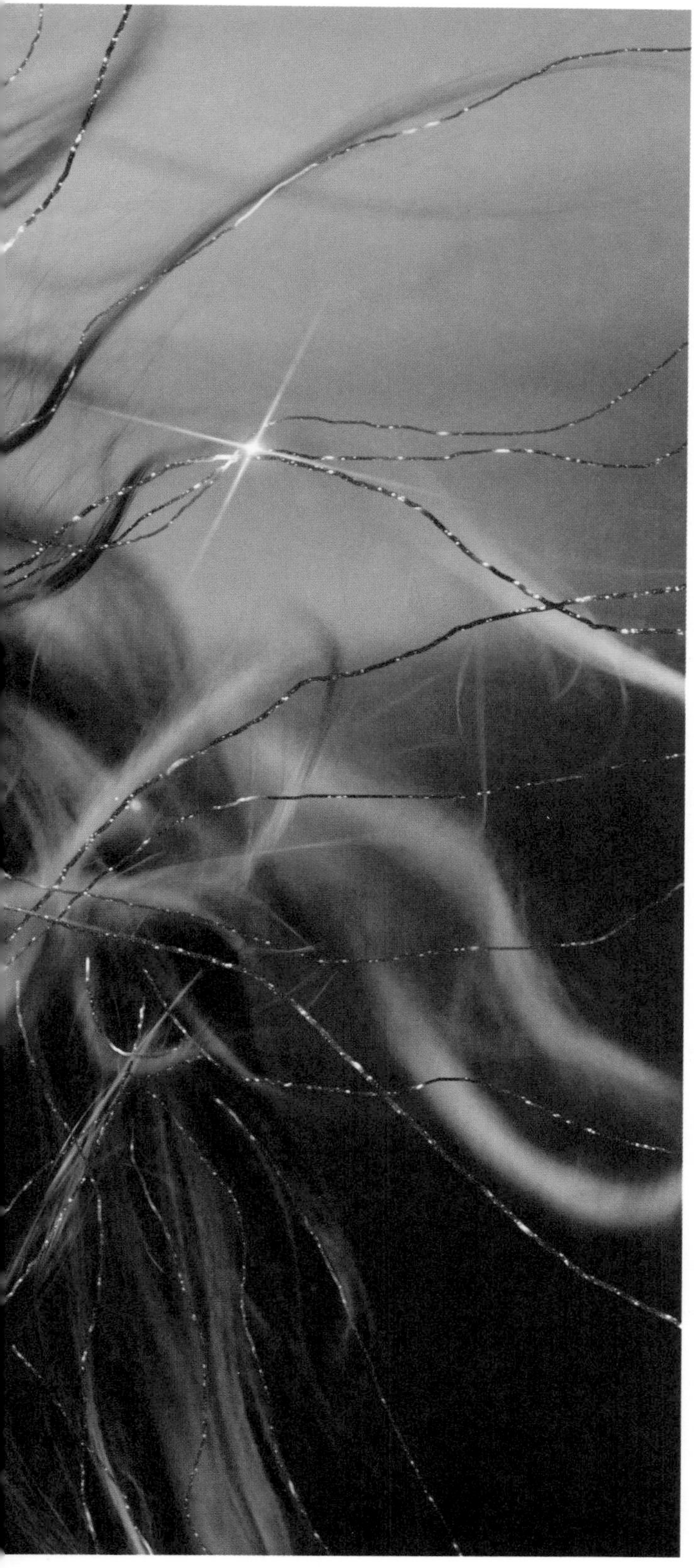

CHAPTER 4

YOUR LUNAR LIFE

Live your best lunar life by using the indexes and resources to guide you towards fixes for worries and dreams associated with each and every aspect of life.

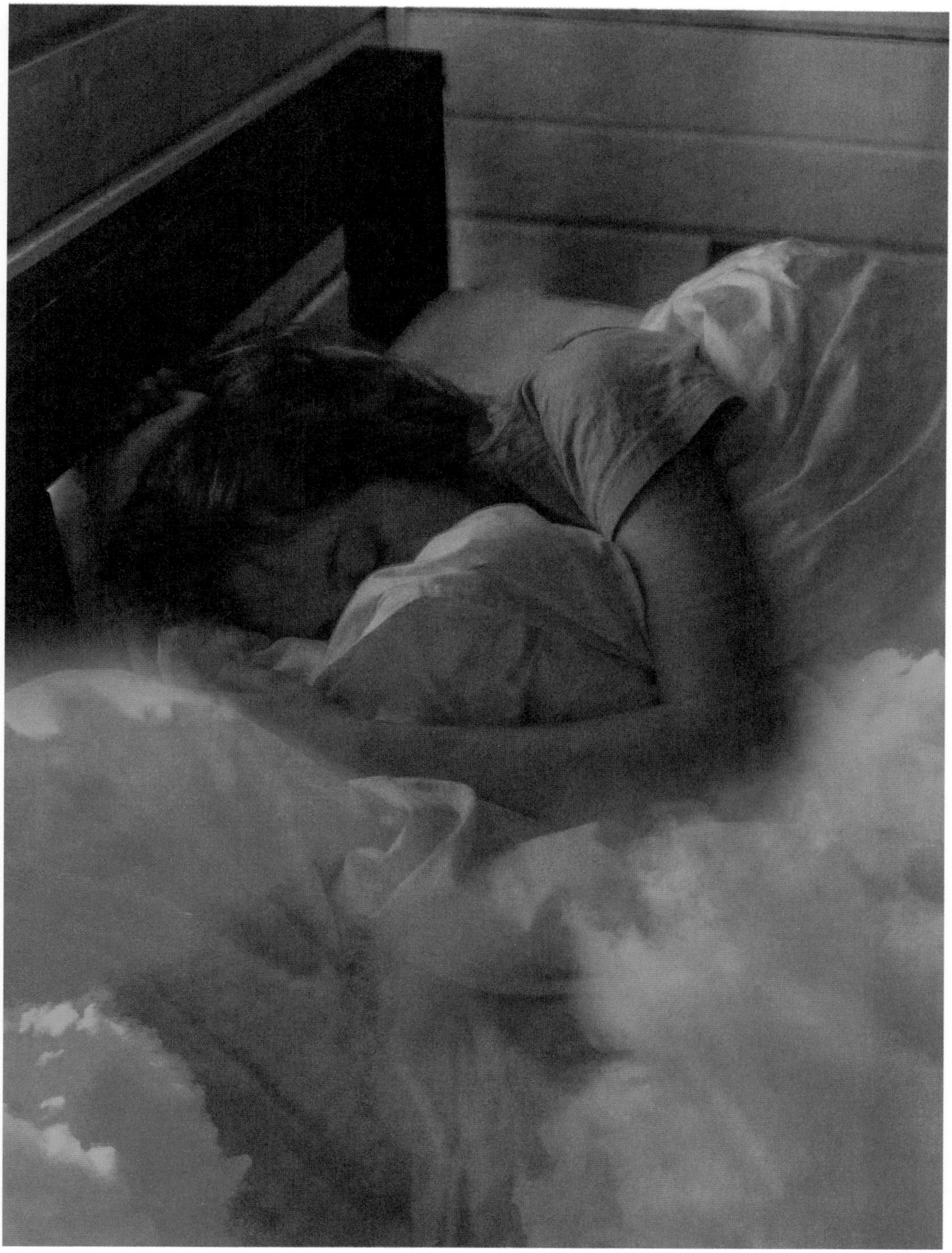

Conclusion
Listening to the Moon

Working with the phases of the moon can help you feel more in tune with the rhythms of your life. Lunar power connects to your intuition or the wise part within you that knows what is in your best interests – the part of you that knows there is always more to this life than meets the eye. If you consider yourself a spiritual being, working with this book can help you keep your feet on the ground as you reach for the moon. Open your body, mind and heart to lunar power and experience the healing and different kinds of magic it can bring into your life.

Start living your lunar-inspired life now. Reread this book. Meditate on all the glorious illustrations. Commit to getting your moon fix every day. If you have a specific worry or dream, use the Index of Fixes by Need on the pages that follow to find relevant moon fixes to help you. If you have any questions or moon stories and insights to share, get in touch with me. Details of how to connect with me and how to join a growing community of moon watchers can be found on page 175.

Moon watching is a truly fulfilling and beautiful way to live.

Thank you for journeying with me a while under the shimmering light of the moon. May she forever watch over you, guide you and light your way.

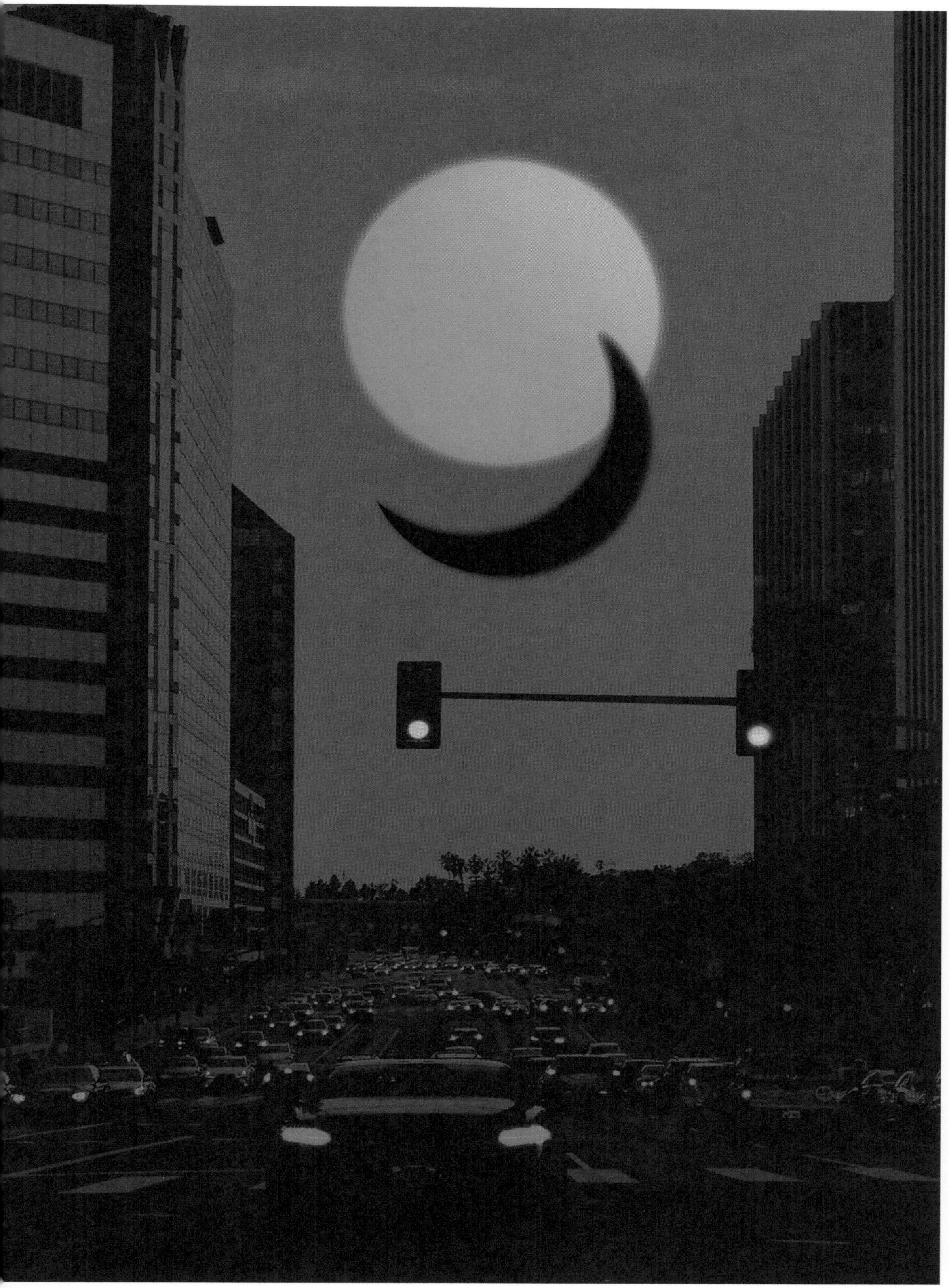

Index of Fixes by Need

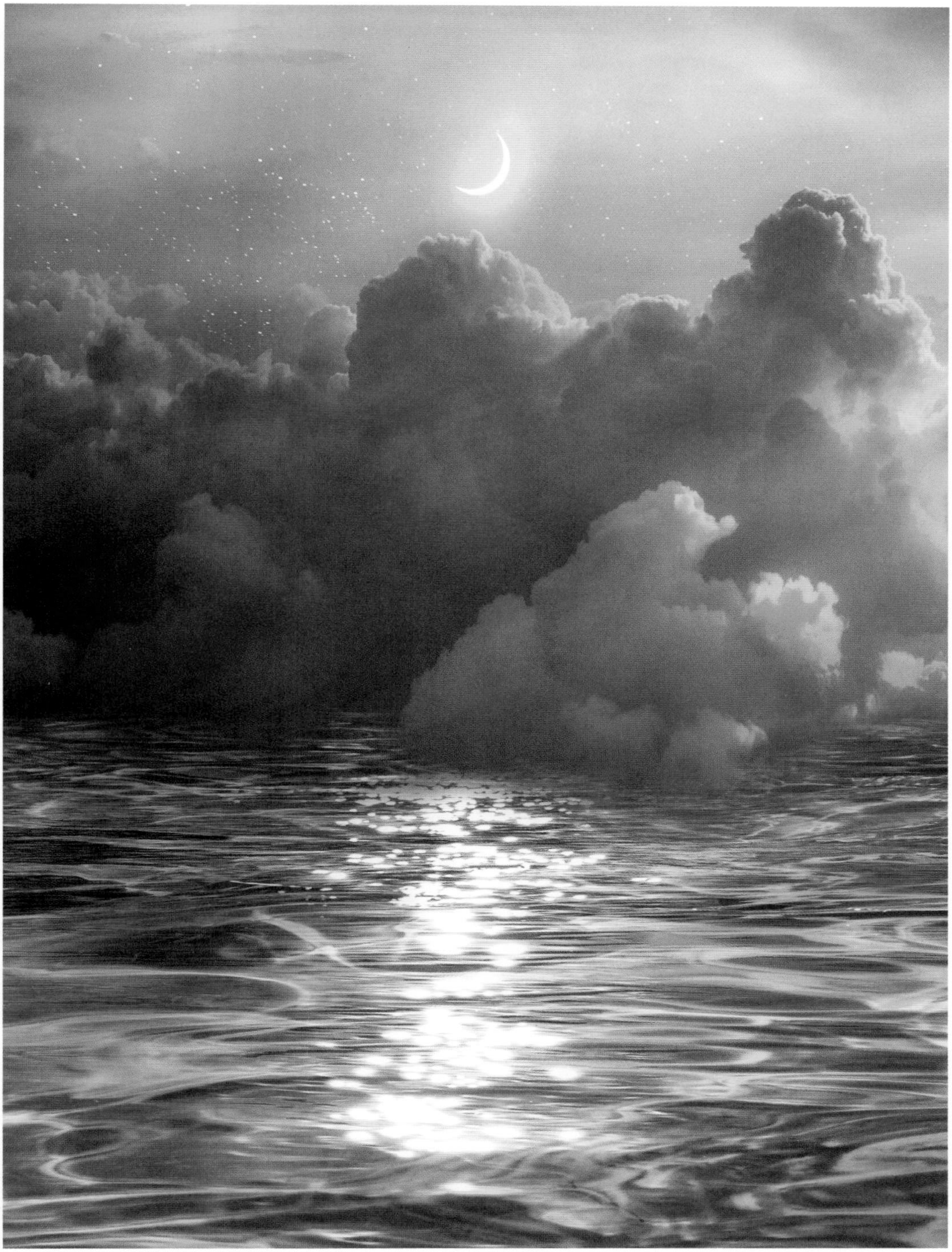

General Index

Further Moon Resources

www.lunarium.co.uk/moonsign/calculator.jsp
Use this section of the Lunarium website if you are interested in researching
further and discovering your moon sign.

www.moonology.com
Astrology resource with a moon-loving component.

www.timeanddate.com/moon/phases
Find out each day which phase the moon is currently in for you.

www.thejourneyjunkie.com/life/how-to-make-a-dreamcatcher/
Learn how to make your own dream catcher (see page 158 for how to use it).

Acknowledgements

Sincere gratitude to my editor, Zara Anvari, for being the illumination behind this book, and to Laura Bulbeck for her invaluable input and inspiration with editing. I'd also like to thank Indigo for the illustrations and everyone at Quarto involved in the publication and promotion of this book . . .

Heartfelt thanks to my incredibly wise agent Jane Graham Maw (www.grahammawchristie.com). Credit also to Ingrid Court Jones for her amazing help with early copy-editing of my material. And last, but by no means least, deepest love and gratitude to Ray, Robert and Ruthie as I immersed myself in the blissful ritual of writing this book by day and, of course, by moonlight.

About the Author

Theresa Cheung, moon sign Cancer, was born into a family of astrologers and psychics. Since leaving King's College, Cambridge, with a degree in Theology and English, she has written numerous popular mind, body and spirit books and encyclopaedias, including two *Sunday Times* Top 10 titles. She has sold well over half-a-million books and her titles have been translated into more than 30 different languages and have become international bestsellers. She has written features on personal growth and spiritual development for magazines and national newspapers as well as being interviewed for both radio and TV. She works closely with scientists studying consciousness and dreams and is collaborating with the Institute of Noetic Sciences (IONS). Theresa's website is www.theresacheung.com.

TALK TO THE MOON To contact Theresa with any moon stories or insights, feel free to reach out to her via her Facebook and Instagram author pages. You can also email her via her website or direct at: angeltalk710@aol.com. Theresa endeavours to reply to everyone who messages her. However, please bear in mind that sometimes it can take her a while to reply when life gets super busy – or if it's a full moon!

Brimming with creative inspiration, how-to projects and useful information to enrich your everyday life, Quarto Knows is a favourite destination for those pursuing their interests and passions. Visit our site and dig deeper with our books into your area of interest: Quarto Creates, Quarto Cooks, Quarto Homes, Quarto Lives, Quarto Drives, Quarto Explores, Quarto Gifts, or Quarto Kids.

First published in 2020 by White Lion Publishing,
an imprint of The Quarto Group.
The Old Brewery, 6 Blundell Street
London, N7 9BH,
United Kingdom
T (0)20 7700 6700
www.QuartoKnows.com

A catalogue record for this book is available from the British Library.

ISBN 978 1 78131 948 2
Ebook ISBN 978 1 78131 949 9
10 9 8 7 6 5 4 3 2 1

Printed in Singapore

MIX
Paper from responsible sources
FSC www.fsc.org FSC® C016973

DISCLAIMER: The information in this book is for informational purposes only and is not intended as a guide to replace the advice of a counsellor, physician or medical practitioner. Some of the views expressed in this book may be controversial and you are encouraged to consult other sources and make independent judgments about the themes and ideas discussed in this book. There is the possibility of allergic or other adverse reactions from the use of any herbs, plants, foods, incense, crystals or essential oils mentioned in this book. You should seek the advice of your doctor or other qualified health provider with any questions you may have, especially if you have a medical condition or are pregnant. This book is not intended for children. You should not use the information in this book as a substitute for contraception, medication or other treatment prescribed by your medical practitioner. Never delay seeking professional medical advice, counselling or therapy because of something you have read in this book.

The authors, editors and publisher make no representations or warranties with respect to the accuracy, completeness, fitness for a particular purpose or currency of the contents of this book and exclude all liability to the extent permitted by law for any errors or omissions and for any loss, damage or expense (whether direct or indirect) suffered by anyone relying on any information contained in this book.